Instructor's Manual

to accompany

CONSTRUCTING LITERACIES

A Harcourt Reader for College Writers

SUSAN BELASCO
University of Nebraska

Course Syllabus and Writing Assignments
Prepared with the Assistance of

T. ALLEN CULPEPPER
Rogers State University

HARCOURT COLLEGE PUBLISHERS

Fort Worth Philadelphia San Diego New York Austin Orlando San Antonio
Toronto Montreal London Sydney Tokyo

ISBN 0-15-507483-0

Copyright (c) 2001 by Harcourt, Inc.

Address for domestic orders:
Harcourt College Publishers
6277 Sea Harbor Drive
Orlando, FL 32887-6777
800-782-4479

Address for international orders:
International Customer Service
Harcourt, Inc.
6277 Sea Harbor Drive
Orlando, FL 32887-6777
407-345-3800
(fax) 407-345-4060
(e-mail) hbintl@harcourt.com

Address for editorial correspondence:
Harcourt College Publishers
301 Commerce Street, Suite 3700
Fort Worth, TX 76102

Web Site Address
http://www.harcourtcollege.com

Printed in the United States of America

0 1 2 3 4 5 6 7 8 9   023   9 8 7 6 5 4 3 2 1

Harcourt College Publishers

CONTENTS

I

TEACHING CONSTRUCTING LITERACIES

OVERVIEW OF THE TEXT

As I note in the Preface to *Constructing Literacies: A Harcourt Reader for College Writers,* the purpose of this textbook is to help students read, think, and write about the multiple literacies that they need for not only negotiating the world of higher education but also for fully participating in an increasingly diverse world. The arrangement of the readings, the questions for discussion, and the suggestions for writing are all designed to encourage students to interact with the text and with the members of their classes. *Constructing Literacies* is informed throughout by a pedagogy based on three key assumptions:

- Writers write best when they are engaged in and involved by their tasks.
- Writing is best undertaken as a process with many opportunities for discussion of ideas, writing and revising drafts, consulting with peers and instructors, and producing well-edited final drafts.
- Students need to learn how to access and use sources of information to be effective readers and writers in the academic world.

This Instructor's Guide is intended as a handbook for teachers using *Constructing Literacies* in their classes. The guide is divided into three parts. In Part I, teachers will find suggestions and examples of teaching strategies for organizing syllabi, using the readings in class discussion, preparing writing assignments, evaluating student work, and holding conferences with students. Part II provides brief synopses of the readings in the text and specific suggestions for discussion and writing assignments. Part III is a list of selected print and electronic resources for teachers.

ADVICE TO WRITING PROGRAM ADMINSTRATORS

One of the advantages of *Constructing Literacies* is that many of the readings and assignments in the text are designed to help students learn about their own college or university campus. Using the text with graduate teaching assistants and instructors who are new to the campus can prompt a sense of camaraderie among students and instructors alike as they learn from the essays and the assignments about the new community they have joined. If a group of instructors are using the text together (or if there is program-wide adoption), a writing program administrator might wish to plan a series of workshops for using the text. Some workshop or discussion session topics might include:

- Constructing a syllabus.
- Conducting classroom discussions.
- Preparing writing assignments.
- Planning a sequence of writing assignments.
- Using readings in the college classroom.
- Meeting the challenge of less-well-prepared students and/or non-native speakers of English.
- Incorporating print and electronic resources in writing assignments.
- Exchanging experiences on effective (and ineffective) strategies in using the text.

I have also found it effective to schedule periodic presentations by various campus staff and administrators, according to the topics of this text. For instance, I always invite the Dean of International Students to speak about the variety of students on campus from year to year; such presentations can help inexperienced instructors become sensitive to the additional demands placed on non-native speakers of English as they learn to negotiate the multiple literacies of a college campus. Additionally, I have reprinted here a variety of forms and evaluation sheets throughout this text that writing program administrators may wish to use or adapt for their own particular circumstances.

ADVICE TO INSTRUCTORS

Constructing Literacies is a text that provides many opportunities for students to learn about their own campuses and engage in the central issues of contemporary higher education. In teaching many of these essays and reports, I have discovered that I can join with the students in learning about our campus and issues of interest to all of us; such a spirit of cooperative inquiry goes a long way toward enlivening class meetings and prompting interesting writing assignments from students. If the content of their writing assignments matters to them, students will be more engaged in what they are doing and will write much more effectively. Spend time talking with your students about their first experiences and impressions of higher education; use their reactions as a departure point for engaging them in the issues raised in the text.

PREPARING TO TEACH

Instructors intending to use *Constructing Literacies* will want to familiarize themselves with the arrangement of the text, the resources available on the Web site, and the information available in this Instructor's Guide. Because many of the reading and writing assignments suggest a preliminary investigation into the student's own college or university resources, instructors will want to investigate the resources of their own institution and the library. How, for example, do students access the online catalogue and the major databases (such as ERIC or Lexis-Nexus)? Instructors will also want to study the college or university Web site. What is the organization of the institution? What resources for students—such as the institutional mission statement—are available online? Instructors may also want to learn how accessible the Internet is on their campuses, the location of computer labs and network connections, and how much technical help is available to students using computers.

Above all, the most effective instructors are those who think of themselves as not only teaching an individual course, but also contributing to the larger goals of a college or university curriculum. In one of the best books, *Teaching Prose,* listed in the third section of this guide, Fredric V. Bogel and Katherine K. Gottschalk wisely observe in the Preface: "Instruction in writing is best accomplished when writing is understood generously rather than narrowly: as a complex of intellectual, rhetorical, and experiential concerns rather than as a set of 'composition skills' isolated from the rest of one's education and dominated by a dread of incorrectness." *Constructing Literacies* is a text designed to uphold that supremely important principle.

ORGANIZATION OF COURSES AND SAMPLE SYLLABI

Whether you are teaching a course according to a program-wide syllabus or designing one of your own, you will need to think carefully about how you will organize your course. Many colleges and universities have requirements about what should go into a syllabus; in general a syllabus for any course should include basic information about the specific instructor (name, office hours, phone number, and e-mail address) and the course (place and time of meeting). In addition, many institutions specify that instructors include information about students who need special services or accommodations and how students in general might locate and receive tutorial help. Beyond that information, a syllabus should include a rationale for the course, which might include a statement about why students should take this course and how the course fits into the university curriculum. A syllabus should also list or summarize the goals of the course.

- What are the objectives for students?
- What is the larger purpose of the course?
- How will different parts of the course help students accomplish the objectives?

A good course syllabus will also provide information to students about the sequence of the course.

- Why is the course arranged the way it is?
- Why have the print or electronic resources listed on the syllabus been chosen and what are students expected to gain from using them in the order they are listed?

Instructor expectations should be clearly outlined.

- What skills do students need to succeed in the course?
- What are the activities in which students are expected to participate?
- If peer editing, collaborative work, and class participation are listed as important activities, how are they defined? How are they evaluated?
- What are the evaluation standards for the course?

A course syllabi should also include specific information about the nature of the reading and writing assignments.

- What is the purpose of each writing assignment?
- How do the readings support the assignments?
- What goals are students expected to accomplish?
- How are the writing assignments evaluated?

Finally, a course syllabus may include a schedule of readings and other assignments or information about how students may find out about due dates for various activities.

SAMPLE SYLLABI

Several syllabi are included here as examples of different ways in which instructors might plan courses using *Constructing Literacies*.

Introduction to College Writing

(SEMESTER)

Course Description

Introduction to College Writing introduces students to strategies and techniques for effective reading, writing, and thinking essential for the student's successful integration into the academic community via participation in the intellectual discourse central to scholarly pursuits at the post-secondary level. The course stresses reading actively, thinking critically, and writing clearly and proficiently for an academic audience, with a particular emphasis on writing as a process involving continual revision. Introduction to College Writing is a hands-on class built on the premise that one learns to write by writing.

Texts and Materials

- *Constructing Literacies: A Harcourt Reader for College Writers* by Susan Belasco (Fort Worth: Harcourt College Publishers, 2001) (Required).
- A portfolio folder (Required).
- A writing handbook and college dictionary (Recommended).

Course Policies and Expectations

Because Introduction to College Writing is a discussion-and-workshop class, it requires the full participation of all students in all class activities. Activities may include (but will not necessarily be limited to) reading, writing, class discussion, online class discussion, group projects, library research, conferences with the instructor, and writing-center tutorials. You will be expected to do a great deal of reading and writing for this class. Prompt and regular attendance and timely submission of assignments are critical both for your success in the class and of the class as a whole; absences and missed deadlines on your part will create problems for your classmates as well. The standards of academic honesty require that you do your own work and only your own work, and that you fully and accurately document any words, thoughts, ideas, information, or work borrowed from others. Violating these policies and expectations will result in appropriate adjustment of your grade for the course. The course will include both traditionally graded assignments and a portfolio-assessment component.

Essential Writing Requirements

- **Five essays with process documentation, each worth 15% of grade.** Each of these essays will be approximately four to five pages long. Each essay assignment will include an outline or planning page, a draft edited by one of your peers, and a revised, graded essay. You must complete all components of each assignment to receive a grade for it. One of the essay assignments (the one on cyberliteracy) will be submitted electronically as an email attachment.

◆ **A portfolio (revised essay, process documentation, process analysis), worth 25% of grade.** Portfolio assessment allows the instructor to evaluate a writing sample reflecting your best work and to assess your understanding and mastery of the writing process. Near the end of the term, you will submit a portfolio folder containing your best revised essay, accompanied by the outline or planning page, drafts, and any other available evidence of the writing process, as well as a process-analysis essay in which you analyze and explain the stages of that process.

Evaluation Criteria

Your papers will be evaluated according to the following criteria:

◆ Clear, argumentative, appropriately placed thesis statement.
◆ Effective introduction and conclusion.
◆ Thorough and perceptive analysis.
◆ Logically organized and effectively supported argument or exposition.
◆ Appropriate language and sentence structure.
◆ Well organized paragraphs with effective transitions between them.
◆ Fluency of thought and language.
◆ Absence of grammatical and mechanical errors.
◆ Adherence to specified format and documentation style.
◆ Evidence of original and perceptive thought.
◆ Adherence to assignment.

Calendar

Week 1: Introduction and assessment. Begin Unit I: "Literacy Narratives." *Reading:* General Introduction, Introduction to Section I, Rose's "I Just Wanna Be Average." *Work focus:* Reading, writing, and thinking for college.

Week 2: "Literacy Narratives" continued. *Reading:* Fishman's "Becoming Literate: A Lesson from the Amish," Zitkala-Sa's "The School Days of an Indian Girl," Douglass's *Narrative*, Malcolm X's "Saved." *Work focus:* Planning for writing, essay structure, drafting essays, audience, and purpose.

Week 3: "Literacy Narratives" concluded. Reading: Rodriguez's "Aria: A Memoir of a Bilingual Childhood," Keller's "The Day Language Came into My Life," Antin's "Initiation," Steiner's "Heraldry." *Work focus:* Mastering rhetorical modes, working with other writers, basic documentation, paragraph development, revising, and editing. *Assignment(s) due:* Essay 1 (on literacy narratives) outline/planning page and draft due for discussion and peer edit.

Week 4: Begin Unit II: "The Purpose of a College Education." *Reading:* Introduction to Section II, [Yale] Committee Report, Hersh's "Intentions and Perceptions." *Work focus:* Rhetorical modes, paragraph unity and coherence, refreshing grammar, punctuation, and mechanics skills. *Assignment(s) due:* Essay 1 revision due for grade (turn in draft and outline along with revision).

Week 5: "The Purpose of a College Education" continued. *Reading:* Edmundson's "On the Uses of a Liberal Education," Nussbaum's "The Old Education and the Think-Academy," Magner's "Professors and Influential Alumni Join Forces to Protect Brooklyn College's Core Curriculum." *Work focus:* Argumentation, thesis statements, drafting, and revision. *Assignment(s) due:* Essay 2 draft due for discussion and peer edit.

Week 6: "The Purpose of a College Education" concluded. *Reading:* Houston's "Bury the Liberal vs. Professional Arts Debate," Schmeiser's "Do Geeks Need to Go to College?" *Work focus:* Finding and evaluating print resources, documentation. *Assignment(s) due:* Essay 2 revision due for grade.

Week 7: Begin Unit III: "Literacies for a Diverse World." *Reading:* Introduction to Section III, Hirsch's "Literacy and Cultural Literacy," Simonson and Walker's "Introduction and Opening the American Mind," and Purves's "General Education and the Search for a Common Culture." *Work focus:* Inductive and deductive reasoning, fallacies, analyzing arguments.

Week 8: "Literacies for a Diverse World" continued. *Reading:* Freire's "The Banking Concept of Education," Moffett's "Censorship and Spiritual Education," Shapiro's "A Parent's Dilemma," and Gates's "The Debate Has Been Miscast from the Start." *Work focus:* Objective observation and analysis of diverse perspective, revising for fairness and completeness. *Assignment(s) due:* Essay 3 draft due for discussion and peer edit.

Week 9: "Literacies for a Diverse World" concluded. *Reading:* Garcia's "Emotional Baggage in a Course on Black Writers," Kidwell's "The Vanishing Native Reappears in the College Curriculum," Cortés's "Pluribus & Unum." *Work focus:* examining assumptions and preconceptions, editing and proofreading effectively, finding and evaluating electronic resources. *Assignment(s) due:* Essay 3 revision due for grade.

Week 10: Begin Unit IV: "Cyberliteracy." *Reading:* Introduction to Section III, Murray's "Lord Burleigh's Kiss," Miller's "www.claptrap.com," and Hunt's "The Cultural Currency of the Book." *Work focus:* Defining and acquiring cyberliteracy, using electronic tools and resources effectively. *Assignment(s) due:* Essay 4 draft due for discussion and peer edit (submitted electronically as email attachment to instructor and peer).

Week 11: "Cyberliteracy" continued. *Reading:* Birkerts's "Perseus Unbound," Roberts's "Virtual Grub Street," and McCollum's "'Ramping Up' to Support 42,000 Student Computers." *Work focus:* Evaluation of electronic tools and resources. *Assignment(s) due:* Essay 4 revision due for grade (submitted electronically as email attachment).

Week 12: "Cyberliteracy" concluded. *Reading:* Oppenheimer's "The Computer Delusion," Himmelfarb's "A Neo-Luddite Reflects on the Internet," Kantrowitz's "Men, Women, and Computers," Tierney's "Women Ease into Mastery of Cyberspace," and Hickman's "Cybercheats: Term-Paper Shopping Online." *Work focus:* Maintaining academic honesty in the computer age.

Week 13: Begin Unit V: "An Education of One's Own." *Reading:* Introduction to Section V, "This Year's Freshmen," "Course-Taking Patterns," Kleinfeld's "Student Performance: Male versus Female." *Work focus:* Developing a process analysis, preparing the portfolio, taking responsibility for one's own education. *Assignment(s) due:* Essay 5 draft due for discussion and peer edit.

Week 14: Break.

Week 15: "An Education of One's Own" concluded. *Reading:* Rhoads's "Gay Liberation and the Passage of the Sexual Orientation Clause," Eitzen's "Big-Time College Sports," Green's "Traditional Degrees, Nontraditional Jobs," and Tompkins's "The Cloister and the Heart." *Work focus:* revising and polishing portofolios, assessment and evaluation, conclusion. *Assignment(s) due:* Essay 5 revision due.

Week 16: *Assignment(s) due:* Final portfolios due for evaluation.

[Note: This syllabus is designed for a 15-week semester with a one-week break and an additional week for final exams (the final portfolio, in this case). For a slightly shorter semester or for a course taught by teaching assistants with their own final exam obligations, the course could be condensed by eliminating a few readings and covering one of the three-week units in two weeks—the "Literacy Narratives" unit at the beginning of the course, for example, could be covered adequately in two weeks.]

Introduction to College Writing

(QUARTER)

Course Description

Introduction to College Writing introduces students to strategies and techniques for effective reading, writing, and thinking essential for the student's successful integration into the academic community via participation in the intellectual discourse central to scholarly pursuits at the post-secondary level. The course stresses reading actively, thinking critically, and writing clearly and proficiently for an academic audience, with a particular emphasis on writing as a process involving continual revision. Introduction to College Writing is a hands-on class built on the premise that one learns to write by writing.

Texts and Materials

- *Constructing Literacies: A Harcourt Reader for College Writers* by Susan Belasco (Fort Worth: Harcourt College Publishers, 2001) (Required).
- A portfolio folder (Required).
- A writing handbook and college dictionary (Recommended).

Course Policies and Expectations

Because Introduction to College Writing is a discussion-and-workshop class, it requires the full participation of all students in all class activities. Activities may include (but will not necessarily be limited to) reading, writing, class discussion, online class discussion, group projects, library research, conferences with the instructor, and writing-center tutorials. You will be expected to do a great deal of reading and writing for this class. Prompt and regular attendance and timely submission of assignments are critical both for your success in the class and of the class as a whole; absences and missed deadlines on your part will create problems for your classmates as well. The standards of academic honesty require that you do your own work and only your own work, and that you fully and accurately document any words, thoughts, ideas, information, or work borrowed from others. Violating these policies and expectations will result in appropriate adjustment of your grade for the course. The course will include both traditionally graded assignments and a portfolio-assessment component.

Essential Requirements

- **Four essays (draft and revision required), each worth 15% of grade.** Each of these essays will be approximately four to five pages long. Each essay assignment will include a draft edited by one of your peers, and a revised, graded essay. You must complete all components of each assignment to receive a grade for it. One of the essay assignments (the one on cyberliteracy) will be submitted electronically as an email attachment.

♦ **A portfolio (consisting of one of your previous essays, revised again and accompanied by a process analysis), worth 30% of grade.** Portfolio assessment allows the instructor to evaluate a writing sample reflecting your best work and to assess your understanding and mastery of the writing process. Near the end of the term, you will submit a portfolio folder containing your best revised essay, accompanied by all drafts, and any other available evidence of the writing process, as well as a process-analysis essay in which you analyze and explain the stages of that process.

♦ **Active participation in class discussion, group projects, and other class activities, worth 10% of grade.**

Evaluation Criteria

Your papers will be evaluated according to the following criteria:

♦ Clear, argumentative, appropriately placed thesis statement.
♦ Effective introduction and conclusion.
♦ Thorough and perceptive analysis.
♦ Logically organized and effectively supported argument or exposition.
♦ Appropriate language and sentence structure.
♦ Well organized paragraphs with effective transitions between them.
♦ Fluency of thought and language.
♦ Absence of grammatical and mechanical errors.
♦ Adherence to specified format and documentation style.
♦ Evidence of original and perceptive thought.
♦ Adherence to assignment.

Calendar

Week 1: Introduction and assessment. "Literacy Narratives." *Reading:* General Introduction, Introduction to Section I, Rose's "I Just Wanna Be Average," Fishman's "Becoming Literate: A Lesson from the Amish," Malcolm X's "Saved." *Work focus:* Reading, writing, and thinking for college, planning for writing, essay structure. *Assignment(s) due:* Essay 1 draft due for discussion and peer edit.

Week 2: "The Purpose of a College Education." *Reading:* Introduction to Section II, [Yale] Committee Report, Hersch's "Intentions and Perceptions," Edmundson's "On the Uses of a Liberal Education." *Work focus:* Essay structure, drafting essays, audience and purpose, rhetorical modes, working with other writers, basic documentation. *Assignment(s) due:* Essay 1 revision due for grade.

Week 3: "The Purpose of a College Education." *Reading:* Nussbaum's "The Old Education and the Think-Academy," Magner's "Professors and Influential Alumni Join Forces to Protect Brooklyn College's Core Curriculum," Houston's "Bury the Liberal vs. Professional Arts Debate," Schmeiser's "Do Geeks Need to Go to College?" *Work focus:* Rhetorical modes, paragraph unity and coherence, refreshing grammar, punctuation, and mechanics skills, paragraph development, revising and editing. *Assignment(s) due:* Essay 2 draft due for discussion and peer edit.

Week 4: "Literacies for a Diverse World." *Reading:* Introduction to Section III, Hirsch's "Literacy and Cultural Literacy," Simonson and Walker's "Introduction and Opening the American Mind," and Purves's "General Education and the Search for a Common Culture," Freire's "The Banking Concept of Education." *Work focus:* Argumentation, thesis statements, drafting and revision, finding and evaluating print resources, documentation. *Assignment(s) due:* Essay 2 revision due for grade.

Week 5: "Literacies for a Diverse World" continued. *Reading:* Moffett's "Censorship and Spiritual Education," Shapiro's "A Parent's Dilemma," Kidwell's "The Vanishing Native Reappears in the College Curriculum," Garcia's "Emotional Baggage in a Course on Black Writers," Cortés's "Pluribus & Unum." *Work focus:* Inductive and deductive reasoning, fallacies, analyzing arguments, objective observation and analysis of diverse perspectives, revising for fairness and completeness. *Assignment(s) due:* Essay 3 draft due for discussion and peer edit.

Week 6: "Cyberliteracy." Reading: Introduction to Section III, Murray's "Lord Burleigh's Kiss," Miller's "www.claptrap.com," Hunt's "The Cultural Currency of the Book." Birkerts's "Perseus Unbound." *Work focus:* Defining and acquiring cyberliteracy, using electronic tools and resources effectively, examining assumptions and preconceptions, editing and proofreading effectively, finding and evaluating electronic resources. *Assignment(s) due:* Essay 3 revision due for grade.

Week 7: "Cyberliteracy." *Reading:* McCollum's "'Ramping Up' to Support 42,000 Student Computers" Oppenheimer's "The Computer Delusion," Himmelfarb's "A Neo-Luddite Reflects on the Internet," Kantrowitz's "Men, Women, and Computers," and Hickman's

"Cybercheats: Term-Paper Shopping Online." *Work focus:* Use and evaluation of electronic tools and resources, maintaining academic honesty in the computer age. *Assignment(s) due:* Essay 4 draft due for discussion and peer edit (submitted to instructor and peer electronically via email attachment).

Week 8: "An Education of One's Own." *Reading:* Introduction to Section V, "This Year's Freshmen," "Course-Taking Patterns," Kleinfeld's "Student   Performance: Male versus Female." *Work focus:* Developing a process analysis, preparing the portfolio, taking responsibility for one's own education. *Assignment(s) due:* Essay 4 revision due for grade (submitted electronically via email attachment.

Week 9: *Reading:* Rhoads's "Gay Liberation and the Passage of the Sexual Orientation Clause," Eitzen's "Big-Time College Sports," Green's "Traditional Degrees, Nontraditional Jobs," and Tompkins's "The Cloister and the Heart." *Work focus:* revising and polishing portfolios, assessment and evaluation, conclusion. *Assignment(s) due:* Final portfolios due for evaluation.

Introduction to College Writing

(ONLINE)

Course Description

Introduction to College Writing introduces students to strategies and techniques for effective reading, writing, and thinking essential for the student's successful integration into the academic community via participation in the intellectual discourse central to scholarly pursuits at the post-secondary level. The course stresses reading actively, thinking critically, and writing clearly and proficiently for an academic audience, with a particular emphasis on writing as a process involving continual revision. Introduction to College Writing is a hands-on class built on the premise that one learns to write by writing. Requirements include reading, writing (five essays—draft and revision), participation in threaded discussion of reading and writing, and participation in peer-editing exercises.

Texts

- *Constructing Literacies: A Harcourt Reader for College Writers* by Susan Belasco (Fort Worth: Harcourt College Publishers, 2001) (Required).
- A writing handbook and college dictionary (Recommended).

Course Policies and Expectations

Because Introduction to College Writing is a discussion-and-workshop class, it requires the full participation of all students in all class activities. Activities may include (but will not necessarily be limited to) reading, writing, participation in threaded discussions, electronic and library research, email conferences with the instructor, and peer-editing exercises conducted via email. You are expected to meet all scheduled deadlines; I do not accept late work. Taking the course online requires competence in computer-based word-processing, sending and receiving email messages and attachments, and navigating the World Wide Web, as well as access to computer hardware and software sufficient to support required tasks. The standards of academic honesty require that you do your own work and only your own work, and that you fully and accurately document any words, thoughts, ideas, information, or work borrowed from others. Violating these policies and expectations will result in appropriate adjustment of your grade for the course.

Essential Requirements

- *Five essays (draft and revision required), each worth 100 points.* Each of these essays will be approximately four to five pages long. Each essay assignment will include a draft edited by one of your peers, and a revised, graded essay. You must complete all components of each assignment to receive a grade for it. Drafts will be submitted electronically by email attachment to the instructor and an assigned peer editor. Revised essays will be submitted electronically by email attachment to the instructor. I will not accept an assignment that reaches me after the specified deadline.

- Active and competent participation in five peer-editing exercises, each worth 30 points.
- Completion of seven study/exercise units (Critical Thinking, Reading and Writing; Essay Structure and Organization; Rhetorical Strategies; Documentation; Argumentation; and Editing and Revision; and Research), each worth 30 points.
- One contribution to the threaded discussion for each reading assignment—28 contributions, each worth 5 points

Total points possible: 1,000

Evaluation Criteria

Your papers will be evaluated according to the following criteria:

- Clear, argumentative, appropriately placed thesis statement.
- Effective introduction and conclusion.
- Thorough and perceptive analysis.
- Logically organized and effectively supported argument or exposition.
- Appropriate language and sentence structure.
- Well organized paragraphs with effective transitions between them.
- Fluency of thought and language.
- Absence of grammatical and mechanical errors.
- Adherence to specified format and documentation style.
- Evidence of original and perceptive thought.
- Adherence to assignment.

Your peer-editing participation will be evaluated on the basis of the thoroughness and conscientiousness with which you editing your peer's writing. Your contributions to the threaded discussion will be evaluated on the basis of their number, thoroughness, relevance, perceptiveness, and timeliness.

Course Outline

The course will be divided into five units. Each unit will include reading, discussion contributions, an essay draft, a peer-editing exercise, and a revised essay.

Unit 1: "Literacy Narratives"

Reading:
    General Introduction
    Introduction to Section I
    Rose's "I Just Wanna Be Average"
    Fishman's "Becoming Literate: A Lesson from the Amish"
    Malcolm X's "Saved"
    Douglass's *Narrative*
    Zitkala-Sa's "The School Days of an Indian Girl"

Discussion: One contribution each for Rose, Fishman, Malcolm X, Douglass, and Zitkala-Sa

Writing: Essay 1 on literacy narratives (I will post the assignment). The essay process includes a draft, a peer-editing session, and a revised essay.

Other assignments: Study/exercise Units 1 (Critical Thinking, Reading, and Writing) and 2 (Essay Structure and Organization).

Unit 2: "The Purposes of a College Education"
Reading:
    Introduction to Section II
    [Yale] Committee report
    Hersh's "Intentions and Perceptions"
    Edmundson's "On the Uses of a Liberal Education"
    Houston's "Bury the Liberal vs. Professional Arts Debate"
    Schmeiser's "Do Geeks Need to Go to College?"

Discussion: One contribution each for Committee Report, Hersh, Edmundson, Houston, and Schmeiser

Writing: Essay 2 on purposes of education (I will post the assignment). The essay process includes a draft, a peer-editing session, and a revised essay.

Other assignments: Study/exercise Units 3 (Rhetorical Strategies) and 4 (Documentation)

Unit 3: "Literacies for a Diverse World"

Reading:
    Introduction to Section III
    Hirsch's "Literacy and Cultural Literacy"
    Simonson and Walker's "Introduction and Opening the American Mind"
    Moffett's "Censorship and Spiritual Education"
    Shapiro's "A Parent's Dilemma"
    Kidwell's "The Vanishing Native Reappears in the College Curriculum"
    Cortés's "Pluribus & Unum"

Discussion: One contribution each for Hirsch, Simonson and Walker, Moffett, Shapiro, Kidwell, and Cortes

Writing: Essay 3 on literacies of diversity (I will post the assignment). The essay process includes a draft, a peer-editing session, and a revised essay.

Other assignments: Study/exercise Units 5 (Editing and Revision) and 5 (Argumentation)

Unit 4: "Cyberliteracy"

Reading:
> Introduction to Section IV
> Miller's "www.claptrap.com"
> Hunt's "The Cultural Currency of the Book"
> Oppenheimer's "The Computer Delusion"
> Kantrowitz's "Men, Women, and Computers"
> Hickman's "Cybercheats: Term-Paper Shopping Online"

Discussion: One contribution each for Miller, Hunt, Oppenheimer, Kantrowitz, and Hickman

Writing: Essay 4 on cyberliteracy (I will post the assignment). The essay process includes a draft, a peer-editing session, and a revised essay.

Other assignments: Study/exercise Unit 7A (Electronic research)

Unit 5: "An Education of One's Own"

Reading:
> Introduction to Section V
> "This Year's Freshmen"
> "Course-Taking Patterns"
> Kleinfeld's "Student Performance: Male versus Female"
> Rhoads's "Gay Liberation and the Passage of the Sexual Orientation Clause"
> Green's "Traditional Degrees, Nontraditional Jobs"

Discussion: One contribution each for "This Year's Freshmen," "Course-Taking Patterns," Kleinfeld, Rhoads, and Green

Writing: Essay 4 on cyberliteracy (I will post the assignment). The essay process includes a draft, a peer-editing session, and a revised essay.

Other assignments: Study/exercise Unit 7B (Print and primary research)

Freshman Seminar
Exploring Academic Literacies
(Semester)

Course Description

The Freshman Seminar allows a relatively small group of first-year students to explore actively topics pertinent to higher education and students' role in it. You will be asked to think, write, and talk about such issues as definition and development of literacy/literacies, the purpose(s) of a college education, diversity in the university and college, cyberliteracy, and making education one's own. The course's primary objective is to help you develop the literacies that you need to understand and negotiate the world of higher education knowledgeably and successfully.

Text

Constructing Literacies: A Harcourt Reader for College Writers by Susan Belasco (Fort Worth: Harcourt College Publishers, 2001).

Course Policies and Expectations

A seminar requires the full participation of all students in all class activities. Activities may include (but will not necessarily be limited to) reading, writing, class discussion, and online class discussion). Prompt and regular attendance and timely submission of assignments are critical both for your success in the class and for the success of the class as a whole. The standards of academic honesty require that you do your own work and only your own work and that you fully and accurately document any words, thoughts, ideas, information, or work borrowed from others. Violating these policies and expectations will result in appropriate adjustment of your grade for the course.

Essential Requirements

+ A response note for each group of readings, 15% of grade.
+ One 500-word essay, 15 % of grade.
+ One 1,000-word essay, 20% of grade.
+ A mid-term test, 15% of grade.
+ A final exam, 25% of grade.
+ Participation, 10 % of grade.

Evaluation Criteria

Journal entries will be evaluated in terms of accuracy, engagement with the reading as evidenced by your critical response to it, and clarity and technical proficiency of writing. Essays will be judged on content, organization, sentence structure (including both fluency and adherence to standard grammar and punctuation), analytical proficiency, argumentation, and depth of critical perception. The mid-term and final will be in short-essay format. The participation grade will depend on significant, sustained, productive, and well articulated contributions to class discussions and other activities.

Calendar

Week 1: Introduction and evaluation. Begin Unit I, "Literacy Narratives." *Reading:* General Introduction, Introduction to Section I, Rose's "I Just Wanna Be Average," Andrea Fishman's "Becoming Literate: A Lesson from the Amish." *Discussion issues:* What are some definitions and implications or literacy/literacies? What does it mean to be literate/illiterate? What exactly is a narrative? Why "narrative" rather than "story" or "myth" or some other similar term? What does any of this have to do with being a first-year college student? *Assignment(s) due:* Response note on readings.

Week 2: "Literacy Narratives" continued. *Reading:* Douglass's "Narrative," Malcolm X's "Saved," Zitkala-Sa's "The School Days of an Indian Girl," and Antin's "Initiation." (Video option: Spike Lee's *Malcolm X*). *Discussion issues:* What are the boundaries of literacy/illiteracy? How do metaphors and analogies of imprisonment vs. freedom function in the discourse of literacy? How does one's insider/outsider status affect one's perceptions of literacy and rhetorical power? How, to whom, and for what purposes do outsiders and insiders speak/write? *Assignment(s) due:* Response note on readings.

Week 3: "Literacy Narratives" concluded. *Reading:* Keller's "The Day Language Came into My Life," Rodriguez's "Aria: A Memoir of a Bilingual Childhood," Minatoya's "Transformation," and Steiner's "Heraldry." *Discussion issues:* What is language? Why is language? Where does it come from? How does it develop? Who acquires it and how? How do you tell which language is the language? What if yours is the wrong one? What if it's the right one? *Assignment(s) due:* Response note on readings. [*Research possibility:* bilingual education. *Reserve reading possibility:* Robert McCrum, William Cran, and Robert MacNeil, *The Story of English* (New York: Penguin, 1987); the PBS series segments are also available on videotape.]

Week 4: Begin Unit II, "The Purpose of a College Education." *Reading:* Introduction to Section II, Committee of the Corporation's *Report*, Hersh's "Intentions and Perceptions." *Discussion issues:* Academically speaking, where did we come from and why are we here? What is college? What are the kinds of colleges and their functions? What is education? Who decides what it is? Why are such decisions made? What are the purposes of college education? Is there one overall purpose of education? Whose purpose is it? Why? What are the strengths/weaknesses and advantages/disadvantages of higher education? What power structures and disruptive forces maintain and/or challenge the educational status quo? *Assignment(s) due:* Response note on readings. [*Reserve reading possibility:* Neil Postman, *The End of Education* (New York: Vintage, 1996).]

Week 5: "The Purpose of a College Education" continued. *Reading:* Booth's two "Is There Any Knowledge" essays, Edmundson's "On the Uses of a Liberal Education," and Nussbaum's "The Old Education and the Think-Academy." *Discussion issues:* What is general knowledge? How do we acquire it? Who should have it and why? Is it different for men and women? Must we always force issues into dualities and dialectics? Does every issue really have two sides? More than two? Who decides what knowledge students need? How has college education in American changed over the years? What are the implications of the changes? What *should* be the purposes of higher education? Who should/shouldn't go to college? *Assignment(s) due:* Response note on readings, 500-word essay on literacy narratives or the purpose(s) of college education.

Week 6: "The Purpose of a College Education" concluded. *Reading:* Magner's "Professors and Influential Alumni Join Forces to Protect Brooklyn College's Core Curriculum," Houston's "Bury the Liberal vs. Professional Arts Debate," Schmesier's "Do Geeks Need to Go to College?" *Discussion issues:* What were/are the liberal arts? Who needs them anyway? What is the function of a college education—general knowledge? Personal development? Career preparation? All/none of the above? What is a canon? What is a core curriculum? Why is it important/unimportant? Should it be maintained, abolished, expanded, narrowed, or what? Why should we care? What difference does it make ultimately? Is college an outmoded concept? Is an online degree a college education? Does it matter whether it is? What are the advantages/ disadvantages of traditional vs. non-traditional educational media and methods? Why are we paying to heat and cool all these ivy-covered buildings if we can buy a cheaper but equally functional degree on the Internet? *Assignment(s) due:* Response note on readings. [*Reserve reading possibility:* David Denby, *Great Books. Research possibility:* Can you/should you get a degree without attending in classes? Try a Web search for distance education options in a particular field.]

Week 7: Begin Unit III: "Literacies for a Diverse World." *Reading:* Introduction to Section III, Hirsch's "Literacy and Cultural Literacy" and " The Appendix List," Simonson and Walker's "Introduction and Opening the American Mind," and Purves's "General Education and the Search for a Common Culture." Discussion issues: What are the similarities/difference between general literacy and specific "literacies"? What does it mean to be literate in a particular culture and/or discipline? Is "common culture" a real possibility or in ideological construct? What does it mean exactly? Is it a goal worth striving for? Why or why not? Is it possible to make a list of what people should know? Has cultural literacy deteriorated, or has it changed in some other way? *Assignment(s) due:* Response note on readings. [Reserve reading possibility: E. D. Hirsch, Jr., *Cultural Literacy* (New York: Houghton, 1987); E. M. Foster, *A Passage to India*.]

Week 8: "Literacies for a Diverse World" continued. *Reading:* Freire's, "The Banking Concept of Education," Barber's "America Skips School," Moffett's "Censorship and Spiritual Education," and Shapiro's "A Parent's Dilemma." *Discussion issues:* What metaphors are education are richest and most useful? What does "banking" have to do with education? How relevant is Barber's "Real-World Cultural Literacy" test? Would paying teachers more really have a significant effect on American education? Why/why not? Who does/should decide what educational material is "appropriate"? How can we deal effectively with the dilemma that Moffett articulates as "a single curriculum for a pluralistic populace"? *Assignment(s) due:* Response note on reading, midterm exam.

Week 9: "Literacies for a Diverse World" concluded. *Reading:* Gates's "The Debate Has Been Miscast from the Start," Garcia's "Emotional Baggage in a Course on Black Writers," Kidwell's "The Vanishing Native Reappears in the College Curriculum," Cortés's "Pluribus & Unum." *Discussion issues:* What exactly *is* the debate? How has it been miscast (if it has)? What kinds of emotional baggage are likely to present themselves in the classroom? How can college courses help students deal with such problems? Who made the native vanish? How and why? Should we be worried? Will we vanish next? How can we deal with the troublesome *e pluribus unum* paradox? Should we stress the *pluribus* or the *unum*? What are the likely consequences of our choice? *Assignment(s) due:* Response note on reading.

Week 10: Begin Unit IV: "Cyberliteracy." *Reading:* Introduction to Section IV, Murray's "Lord Burleigh's Kiss," Miller's "www.claptrap.com," and Hunt's "The Cultural Currency of the Book." Discussion issues: How can we define "cyberliteracy"? How does it resemble/differ from other "literacies"? Does it level boundaries are merely create different ones? Can we live without it? Should it scare us a little? From an academic perspective, is the Web a research boon or electronic trash? The Internet: Where can we take it, and when should we leave it? How can we evaluate Internet materials effectively? [*Discussion suggestion:* These issues could be debated effectively online, via discussion group, threaded discussion, listserv, email, etc. *Research suggestion:* Gather examples of Web resources that would be acceptable/unacceptable academic sources. An ambitious group of students with sufficient time could construct and publish a Web page containing a user's guide to Internet materials.] *Assignment(s) due:* Response note on readings.

Week 11: "Cyberliteracy" continued. *Reading:* Birkerts's "Perseus Unbound," Roberts's "Virtual Grub Street," and McCollum's "'Ramping Up' to Support 42,000 Student Computers." Discussion issues: What are the advantages/disadvantages of computers as writing spaces? What is the relationship between electronic resources and books? Can we keep up with technology? Have we gone virtually insane? Do we use technology, or does it use us? *Assignment(s) due:* Response note on reading.

Week 12: "Cyberliteracy" concluded. Reading: Oppenheimer's "The Computer Delusion," Himmelfarb's "A Neo-Luddite Reflects on the Internet," Kantrowitz's "Men, Women, and Computers," Tierney's "Women Ease into Mastery of Cyberspace," and Hickman's "Cybercheats: Term-Paper Shopping Online." Are we deluded about computers? If so, how, and what can we do to rid ourselves of our delusions? Are men and women in general at different stages of computer literacy? If so, what cultural or behavioral factors might explain the discrepancy? How much of a problem is academic fraud involving the Internet? How did the Internet get from where it started to where it is? *Assignment(s) due:* Response note on reading.

Week 13: Begin Unit V: "An Education of One's Own." *Reading:* Introduction to Section V, "This Year's Freshmen," Gose's " 'U. of Chicago Social Life' May No Longer Be an Oxymoron," Green's "Traditional Degrees, Nontraditional Jobs," and Eitzen's "Big-Time College Sports." What are first-year students really like? Should education attempt to cater to them or transform them? Who needs a social life anyway? What consequences do "big-time" sports have for colleges and their students? What should be the relationship between education and career? *Assignment(s) due:* Response note on reading, 1,000 word essay related to diverse literacies, cyberliteracy, or making education one's own.

Week 14: Break.

Week 15: "An Education of One's Own" concluded. *Reading:* "The Absence of Girls in the Current Debate on Education" and "Achievement and Participation," "Course-Taking Patterns," Kleinfeld's "Student Performance: Male versus Female," Rhoads's "Gay Liberation and the Passage of the Sexual Orientation Clause," and Tompkins's "The Cloister and the Heart." *Discussion issues:* How do the academic backgrounds, needs, and performances of female students compare/contrast with those of male students? What implications do gay liberation and sexual-orientation have for queer and straight students? *Assignment(s) due:* Response note on reading. Conclusions.

Week 16: Final exam.

Introduction to College Course

Many colleges and universities provide courses for students that combine advising with an introduction to college life and work. *Constructing Literacies* can be easily used in such a course, supplemented with materials from the student's school.

The College Experience

"The College Experience" provides a forum for reading about, writing about, and discussing the transition from the secondary educational experience to the more rigorous demands of the higher education community. The course addresses the academic, social, and psychological adjustments necessary for students' success, with a particular emphasis on understanding and participating in academic discourse. Required of all first-year students, the course meets weekly throughout the semester for one hour of college credit. Course requirements include attendance, participation in discussion, short writing assignments, quizzes, and a journal in which students respond to reading assignments and to their own experiences of college life.

Required Text

Constructing Literacies: A Harcourt Reader for College Writers by Susan Belasco (Fort Worth: Harcourt College Publishers, 2001).

Required Work

Participation (in discussion and in-class exercises): 20% of grade.
Journal: 30% of grade.
Three short essays: 30% of grade.
Quiz average: 20% of grade.

Calendar

Week 1: Introductory discussion: What does it mean to be literate in the college community?

Week 2: Literacy narratives. Read Rose and Fishman. Quiz. Discussion of reading. Discussion of student experiences: Where did we come from, and how did we get here? Journal entry due.

Week 3: Literacy narratives cont. Read Malcolm X and Zitkala-Sa. Quiz. Discussion of reading. Discussion of student experiences. Essay 1 due.

Week 4: The purpose of a college education. Read Yale Report and Hersh. Quiz. Discussion of reading. Discussion of student experiences: Why are we here? Journal entry due.

Week 5: The purpose of a college education cont. Read Edmundson and Schmeiser. Quiz. Reading discussion. Discussion of student experiences. Essay 1 due.

Week 6: Literacies for a diverse world. Read Gates and Garcia. Quiz. Discussion of reading. Discussion of student experiences: How do we differ from/resemble the others who are here? Journal entry due.

Week 7: Literacies for a diverse world cont. Read Kidwell and Cortes. Quiz. Discussion of reading. Discussion of student experiences.

Week 8: Cyberliteracy. Read Murray, Miller, and Hunt. Quiz. Discussion of reading. Discussion of student experiences: How can we integrate ourselves literately into a virtual community? Journal entry due.

Week 9: Cyberliteracy cont. Read Oppenheimer, Tierney, and Hickman. Quiz. Discussion of reading. Discussion of student experience. Essay 2 due.

Week 10: An education of one's own. Read "This Year's Freshmen," Gose, and Rhoads. Quiz. Discussion of reading. Discussion of student experiences: How do we take control of our own education and find our niche in the academic community? Journal entry due.

Week 11: An education of one's own cont. Read Kleinfeld, Eitzen, and Green. Quiz. Discussion of reading. Discussion of student experiences.

Week 12: An education of one's own cont. Read Tompkins. Quiz. Discussion of reading. Discussion of student experiences. Essay 3 due.

Week 13: Break: No class meeting.

Week 14: Concluding discussion and reflection on the semester.

Week 15: Reading week. No class meeting.

Week 16: Finals week. No class meeting. No final in this class.

SUGGESTIONS FOR TEACHING ACTIVITIES

READINGS

As any experienced instructor will tell you, creating an environment for discussion is the first step toward successful use of readings in any course. Beginning with the first class meeting and even before assigning any readings, try to set a positive, relaxed example to students by asking questions and indicating that you will not be providing all the answers in class. Another important method is to begin class discussions *before* the class begins. One method is to assign questions to students ahead of time and ask for written answers as "homework" to be submitted or brought to class. In *Constructing Literacies,* many of the "Questions for Reading" at the beginning of each selection can be used for this purpose, especially since they are designed to help students combine information they already with what they will learn through their reading. The responses to the questions can be used at the beginning of the class to get the discussion underway. Other techniques may work even more effectively. As the class meeting begins, invite students to look over a specific section of a reading, or asking students to begin the class by writing for two or three minutes in response to a question related to the overall impression of the reading. In *Constructing Literacies,* many of the "Questions for Reaction and Discussion" following each reading can be effectively used for very short, in-class writing assignments. Allow the students to write for a specific amount of time and then either call on students for their responses or pick up the papers and read from them yourself. Use the "Questions for Reading" and the Questions for Reaction and Discussion" in *Constructing Literacies* to help formulate your own provocative questions for use in setting the stage for classroom discussions.

After a discussion is underway in a class, keep it moving along by listening carefully and asking follow-up questions. Invite students in the class to comment on the answers. Try to develop questions beginning with "how" and "why." In necessary, make running notes of student comments on a chalkboard to aid students in thinking aloud and together. Above all, assist students in formulating positions and conclusions by stopping to provide occasional summaries of the discussion and suggest areas that need additional analysis. If the discussion begins to veer from the relevant topic, reintroduce the direction that was originally undertaken, feign forgetfulness, and/or stop the discussion and ask for a summary of the major points made so far.

Good class discussion depend on a variety of contributions for class members. Create the impression that class participation is important and expected. Learn the names of the students in your class and call on silent ones from time to time. Many instructors permit students to "pass" once each class meeting; that can be a very effective technique for helping students understand that speaking up in class is a part of their responsibility. Every instructor has experiences with students who try to monopolize discussions. Remember that not every hand must be acknowledged. Reinforce the idea that class discussion is an expectation for every student in the class. Respond to repeated comments by suggesting that others have not had a chance to respond. If a student seems especially obtuse and refuses to allow others time to speak, take her or him aside after class and ask for help in encouraging others to speak.

Ending a class discussion effectively is as important as beginning it well. Provide some summary statements by asking students to comment on what the class has concluded or observed. Tie the discussion into the broader concerns of the course. Finally, suggest ways in which the discussion of this class meeting prepares the way for the next one.

WRITING ASSIGNMENTS

The first principle of designing effective writing assignments is to have an understanding of the general level of writing abilities of the members of your class. For that reason, I always ask for a short writing sample on the first or second class meeting, depending on how often the class meets and for how long. For example, if my class meets three times a week for 50 minutes, I may use the first class meeting to discuss the syllabus for the course and the second meeting for an in-class writing assignment. But if my class meets twice a week for a longer time, I generally ask for a writing sample on the first day. I make it clear to students that these will be ungraded writing assignments, and I explain that I am using them to collect information about the general level of writing abilities in this specific class.

Two effective in-class writing assignments are given here as examples. In both, students are invited to use information they already possess and are given suggestions about how to structure their answers. Responses to these assignments will help an instructor make a preliminary diagnosis about the level of writing abilities in a class and can provide good information about how to design and sequence the formal writing assignments in the class. Note that both these assignments are timed; the purpose of this assignment is to provide indicators to instructors about writing abilities—not the whole picture.

The first example asks students to use their own educational experience as the basis for their writing.

Diagnostic In-Class Writing Assignment

Read the following two or three times *before* you begin to write. You will have 40 minutes in which to complete this assignment. The quality of what you write is more important than the quantity; your task is to show how clearly and effectively you can write in a short time.

As a recent high school (or the equivalent) graduate, you have been asked to serve on a committee of former students to make recommendations to improve the quality of secondary education in your community. The chair of the committee has asked everyone to write an essay about his or her experiences and make some recommendations for change and improvement. More specifically, the chair has asked that committee members choose a single subject area (like English or history) or one of the requirements for graduation (such as physical education). Briefly describe how this subject area or requirement was organized at your school and then discuss the strengths and weaknesses of the program. This is not an essay about the evaluation of a particular teacher, but you may wish to describe how the courses were taught. Finally, suggest how this part of your education could have been improved.

A second example provides students the written remarks of another for writing:

Diagnostic In-Class Writing Assignment

In "How I Got My Degree at the University of Planet Earth," William Upski Wimsatt writes about his disillusionment with formal post-secondary education and his decision to drop out of college to pursue a "degree" at the "University of Planet Earth." He explains his decision this way:

> When I returned to Oberlin [College] that fall [after a summer vacation and after reading *The Teenage Liberation Handbook: How to Quit School and Get a Real Life and Education*], I realized that there were no courses covering the things I most wanted to learn. No sex classes. No friendship classes. No classes on how to build an organization, raise money, navigate a bureaucracy, create a database, buy a house, love a child, spot a scam, ask the right questions, talk someone out of suicide, or figure out what's important. Those are the things that enhance or mess up people's lives, not whether they know economic theory or can analyze literature.

> So I quit college and enrolled as a student at the University of Plan-
> et Earth, the world's oldest and largest educational institution. It has
> billions of professors, tens of millions of books, and unlimited course
> offerings. Tuition is free, and everybody designs his or her own major.
> (50)
>
> Although you might concede some of Wimsatt's points, your presence
> here at *X College or the University of X* suggests that do not agree with
> him entirely, that you think a formal college education constitutes a
> worthwhile use of your time.
>
> Your assignment is to write a brief essay in which you explain how
> and why you disagree with Wimsatt. Be as specific as possible, and be
> sure to explain what advantages you think a formal college education
> can have over the kind of informal education that Wimsatt has chosen.
>
> Read the topic a couple of times to make sure that you understand
> it and what it asks you to do, and think before you write. This is a short
> assignment in which the clarity and effectiveness of your writing are
> more important than how much you write. You have 30 minutes to com-
> plete your essay.
>
> *Work Cited*
>
> Wimsatt, William Upski. "How I Got My Degree at the University of Planet
> Earth." *Utne Reader,* May–June 1998: 50+.

After an instructor has made some preliminary judgments about the level of
writing abilities in his or her class, he or she can begin to plan a sequence of
writing assignments for the semester. There are a number of excellent books
specifically designed to help instructors design writing assignments, and these
are listed in Part III, Books, Articles, and Bookmarks for the Instructor. But
generally speaking, the best advice that most experienced instructors offer can
be summarized easily. Following the list of principles are some sample writing
assignments, based on the readings in *Constructing Literacies.*

1. Explain the purpose for each assignment and identify the audience
    the students should address. Students are always grateful to have
    concise explanations for why they are being asked to do what they
    are being asked to do. Generally speaking, I encourage students to
    write for the members of their class. I don't use assignments that
    specify audiences (such as the local Rotary Club) because I doubt
    that my students have much experience with Rotarians. I have found
    the best results in explaining to students that they are writing for
    each other; in this way, they have a clear sense of who their audience
    is and how they might better appeal to that audience.

2. Give clear directions about the form of each writing assignment and give the writing assignment in writing. If students are to *summarize* a report they have read and *evaluate* its conclusions, they should know what those terms mean and be given clear directions on how to write a summary and an evaluation. Providing assignments in writing is extremely useful for students as a way to refer to their directions and provides some insurance that students will write on the assignment at hand instead of tangential issues.

3. Explain how each writing assignment will be evaluated. If you expect students to use electronic resources in a writing assignment, you should note that expectation and make it clear that it will be a part of the total evaluation of the assignment. If you expect drafts and notes to be included with a final paper, remind students that those ancillary materials will be a part of the overall evaluation.

4. Provide students some suggestions about how to approach the topic at hand. If students will be able to address your assignment better by studying a related reading or by recalling an earlier assignment, make that clear in the directions. If students are expected to construct an argument, spend some time in class explaining how to do that and on the assignment sheet as well .

5. Provide a timetable for completion of assignments. I find this especially important with first-semester freshmen who may need additional assistance in scheduling their time. Having some intermediate dates for the completion of drafts will underscore the principle that writing is a process of writing, rewriting, and revision, and may also enable students to balance their work in your class with their work in others.

6. Design writing assignments as a sequence and connect the assignments to others in the course. I often begin a new writing assignment by reminding students what they accomplished in their last assignment and drawing on skills they learned there. *Constructing Literacies* is arranged with literacy narratives first and moves to more complex forms such as reports and formal essays. The underlying idea is that students learn best by starting with familiar styles and gaining the confidence to move into more challenging readings and writing assignments.

Sample Writing Assignment

The example is designed as a writing assignment for early in the course, using the selection from Mike Rose's *Lives on the Boundary*. Note how the various principles (printed in **bold**) of writing assignment design are incorporated here.

English 1033.11—Professor Belasco

WRITING ASSIGNMENT 1

As preparation for this writing assignment, you must first complete your reading of Mike Rose's "I Just Wanna Be Average," in *Constructing Literacies*. [Explanation of Preliminary Activity to Be Completed]

In "I Just Wanna Be Average," Mike Rose uses striking examples from his own experiences to provide evidence for the points he wants to make about American education. In an essay of three or four double-spaced pages [Specified Length] discuss the implications of Rose's example of the student (Ken Harvey in the Voc.Ed. religion class) who just wants to be "average."

Suggestion for Approach In this essay, your task is to consider whether just wanting to be "average" is an inevitable circumstance in which some American students find themselves. Use Rose's example as a departure point (and just for practice, include at least two quotations from the book in your paper) and discuss this example from your own educational experience, including the experience you wrote about in your diagnostic essay

Tie to an earlier assignment or other experiences you may have had in school with tracking or placement of student s according to a perceived ability level. You don't need to prove Rose right or wrong; in this essay your task is exploratory. We are taking an idea from Rose's book, checking it against our own experiences, and then considering the implications. [Purpose of the Assignment]

Your essay will be evaluated on the basis of your accurate and careful reading of Rose, your ability to integrate at least two quotations from the book into your paper, your organization, and the appropriateness of your own examples. Final evaluation of the paper will include your rough draft as well as your contribution to the class discussion and to the peer group workshop session. [Evaluation Criteria]

Your final paper is to be typed or printed, double-spaced, and submitted in a folder with your draft and notes attached. We will discuss how to handled quotations from the reading in class. [Format for Essay]

Suggested timetable with activities given for completing essay

Sept. 3—Begin Assignment.

Sept. 8—Draft due; class discussion.

Sept. 10—Peer group review.

Sept. 15—Writing Assignment #1 due in class.

Other examples of writing assignments follow the discussions of the five sections of *Constructing Literacies*.

JOURNALS

Many instructors find that having students keep and use a writing journal throughout the course is an effective way of helping students learn to use writing to think through the issues of the course. To me, the first rule of using journals in class is that they should be guided by course objectives. Too often students are unclear about what the purpose of a journal is; instructors should think hard about what goals students can accomplish by keeping a journal. Instructors will also need to decide whether they want students to keep journals in files on their computers or in notebooks (or both). Journals can be used for both writing in class and outside of class. To be most effective, instructors must comment on student journals from time to time, by integrating them into class discussions and even writing assignments. Most instructors who use journals do not grade them in traditional manners—that is, they do not give formal grades to every entry the students make. However you decide to evaluate a journal, make sure students understand what the criteria is and how the journal fits into the overall evaluation scheme for the course.

Some specific uses for journals can include:

- Pre-writing activities such as summarizing parts or all of the readings, raising questions about the issues presented, and/or detailed responses to individual readings.
- Rehearsals of timed, in-class writing assignments.
- Keep lists of ideas or questions about class discussions and reading assignments.
- Focused free writing activities in which students are asked to write continuously in response to a discussion or reading.
- Try out possible answer to the Questions for Reaction and Discussion at the end of the readings in *Constructing Literacies*.

COLLABORATIVE GROUPS AND PEER WORKSHOPS

I think students benefit enormously from group activities in first-year courses. Instructors can help students learn how to work effectively in groups by creating a positive climate for the work, planning carefully, helping students organize their groups, assigning clear tasks for groups to accomplish, and providing assistance and feedback. Many of the Questions for Writing and the Questions for Further Explorations at the end of the reading selections in *Constructing Literacies* suggest group activities for collecting information and even for collaborative writing assignments.

Using peer groups for revision and even editing activities is a very effective way to encourage students to get involved with the writing of their classmates and to understand the various ways that assignments can be approached. Activities for a peer group can include reading drafts, responding orally and discussing drafts, and providing written comments for the writers. One method is to divide students into revision groups on the day that a draft of an essay is due. Although groups can be voluntarily assembled or assigned, I prefer to assign groups myself, to ensure a good balance of abilities among the students in the groups. Three to four students in a group is the best size, especially if the instructor intends for each student to read all of the drafts in a group. It is very important to train students to read and comment on the work of others. I like to show examples of work in progress and demonstrate how comments can be helpful—or not. Ask them to read each other's drafts and complete a form that has been devised for each assignment. The example below is the basis on which I construct various forms for different assignments.

College Writing

PEER EVALUATION, WRITING ASSIGNMENT #4

1. Thesis

In a single sentence, explain the thesis of the essay you have just read.

2. Sentences

Choose an example of an outstanding sentence in the essay and explain why you think it's unusually good. On the basis of this example, are there suggestion you might make about others?

3. Paragraphs

    A. Check each paragraph. Is there a main idea or a topic sentence in each? Are there any paragraphs that seem to include irrelevant or unnecessary information? Which ones?

    B. Check the transitions between paragraphs. Does each one lead into the next? Are there any places where the transition could be improved? How?

4. Organization

    A. Does the introduction work effectively, that is, does it give the reader a clear idea of the central argument of the essay? If not, how could it be improved?

    B. Is the conclusion effective? Does it merely summarize the main ideas or does it make the final point of the essay stronger and easier to remember?

    C. Does the writer present a strong argument and support it well?

5. Opinion

Are you convinced or persuaded by this essay? Why or why not? Where do you think the writer could provide additional information, details, or examples?

6. Editing: Grammar, Usage, and Mechanics

Are there any places in the essay where your reading is difficult because of various stylistic problems? Which passages in particular?

After students have worked in their groups and completed the comment sheets, ask them to discuss what they learned in general from reading the works of others. Take a look at the comment sheets and help students evaluate the comments they have received.

USING STUDENT WRITING IN CLASS

There are a number of ways to use student writing in class. First and foremost, instructors should tell students at the beginning of the course that they intend to share parts of class members writing with everyone, as a part of the general procedure for the class. Instructors who wish to print and distribute entire essays (or publish papers on Web sites) should get written permission from students *before* they use student essays in this way. Instructors can make up a simple permission form in which students agree to allow their work to be used; both instructor and student can then sign the form.

Informal use of student work falls into a different category; I often tell students that I will be using sentences and paragraphs from their papers from time to time, in order to provide fresh examples. Occasionally, I make up a list of editorial problems, "Peaks and Valleys from a Recent Writing Assignment," and use sentences or phrases from student essays to demonstrate various points I want to make, such as a continual punctuation problem that is cropping up, diction errors and "opportunities" (as I call them), and sentences that simply need revision in one way or another. Sometimes I simply provide a list of all the titles that students used for essays on a particular assignment and direct the discussion to the importance of titles and what they reveal (or obscure.) Occasionally I focus on thesis ideas and reproduce a series of thesis statements or paragraphs that will lead to discussion in class.

Finally, I think it is an excellent idea to use or read student responses in class—or to post them to a Web site for class members to read. I always choose at least two papers (usually two different, equally effective) responses to the same assignment and duplicate them or read them in class when I am returning papers. Students need to know that classmates can and do respond well to assignments, and they need to see the responses of their peers to the issues being discussed in class.

HELPING STUDENTS USE SOURCES FAIRLY

One of the essays in *Constructing Literacies* is a commentary on the availability of research papers for purchase online. John Hickman, the author of the article, observes that professors can help students avoid this by doing more individual work with students and argues for a smaller teacher–student ratio. Recently there has been a proliferation of Web sites designed to help instructors determine whether a student has plagiarized a paper:

www.plagiarism.org

www.canexus.com

www.cs.berkeley.edu/~aiken/moss.html

These sites are designed to search and check papers for similarities to others on the Internet.

I have always felt, however, that an instructor's major job is to educate the innocent first. To this end, I suggest some principles that may help instructors provide assignments that will be hard to plagiarize and at the same time, provide students some necessary guidelines.

1. Give students a list of potential topics or a choice of a small number of assignments that are changed from semester to semester.
2. Take time to discuss the issue of plagiarism and the implications in class.
3. Plan time in class for discussion of papers and research in progress.
4. Require supporting writing assignments as a part of the project—short summaries of outside sources and annotated lists of works consulted.
5. Make time for peer review in class—in advance of the due dates of assignments.
6. Provide models of papers that include sources used well and poorly in class. Discuss the problems and solutions involved in using sources—and the mechanics of using sources fairly and accurately.
7. After students turn in papers, ask them to write a short summary and assessment of their work as an in-class essay.

SPOTTING STUDENTS WHO NEED ADDITIONAL ASSISTANCE

Experienced instructors learn to notice students who are struggling in their classes as early as possible. Some of the selections in *Constructing Literacies* may actually encourage at-risk students to identify themselves in the written or oral comments they make on their reading. While some students will volunteer the information that they need tutoring or wish to know the hours of the Writing Center right away, others may have more difficulty in understanding that they need assistance. Some students come to a college or university campus ill-prepared to write, even in introductory courses, because of limited background on a variety of topics, geographical origin, religious upbringing, and educational experiences. These students may need additional time to become familiar with the environment of higher education. Some other signs to notice are students who habitually seem unable to understand an assignment or know how to begin. These students typically have difficulty in completing pre-writing activities and exercises. Some students may seem unusually nervous about writing under time constraints in class. Students who have a difficult time in understanding why they receive poor grades or what their weaknesses in writing are may not have a sufficient understanding of what constitutes college-level writing and what the role of an instructor is in evaluating their writing. In all cases, students who are struggling in a writing course need some individual attention by the instructor. Inviting the student to an office hour, sending the student an e-mail message asking about progress on an assignment, and/or talking with the student outside of class may make a great deal of difference in assisting a student in getting the help he or she needs to succeed in the course.

STUDENT CONFERENCES

Individual conferences with students can be very valuable as a way to get to know students in a class and to provide additional instruction to students. Some instructors like to schedule a minimum of two conferences with each student during the semester; I prefer to require one and then allow further conferences to develop as needed. The most effective conferences involve a discussion of an assignment in progress; instructors can intervene with students who are having difficulty deciding on a topic, an approach, or ways of developing an assignment. In any case, I always recommend that instructors inform students that they should have an agenda for a conference and to encourage students to come with questions or problems to discuss. Students should understand that arranged conferences with instructors are important appointments.

More recently, I have found e-mail exchanges to form another kind of student conference. Students who may be reluctant to visit an instructor's office will often feel comfortable e-mailing a question or explaining a problem they are having in developing an idea. In any case, holding conferences with students is an effective way of extending the classroom experience.

EVALUATION AND GRADING

To many instructors, grading papers is all about providing detailed comments—writing almost as much as the student has written. A great deal of research in evaluation has clearly shown that students generally do not read and frequently don't understand comments that instructors write on their papers. As many researchers have found, students find numerous comments overwhelming and confusing. The best advice I know about evaluation and grading is written by Maxine Hairston:

> We all know that students must have instruction in writing and feedback on their writing in order to become better writer. . . . But we must focus on ways to given them quality instruction and qualify feedback rather than overwhelming them with more advice than they can absorb and more criticism than they can tolerate. We need to realize that there is not necessarily a positive correlation between our success as writing teachers and the amount of time we spend grading our papers. What we do with students in class before they write and as they write may help them far more than any number of comments after the fact. And creating a positive environment that makes them want to write may turn out to be the most important thing we ever do for them. ("On Not Being a Composition Slave," in *Training the New Teacher of College Composition.* Ed. Charles W. Bridges. Urbana, IL: NCTE, 1986, p. 124.)

With that advice in mind, instructors might begin the process of evaluation with the writing assignment itself, making the criteria for evaluation a part of the written statement of the assignment, as in the examples of writing assignments given in this Instructor's Guide. In addition, instructors might consider providing examples and models of student writing or written statements about what an instructor expects an A paper to accomplish, and on down the line.

Once a student has submitted a final draft of a paper, the instructor's job is to provide meaningful evaluation and comment. A number of the books in Part III of this Instructor's Guide list resources that will help; among the best is Erika Lindemann's *A Rhetoric for Writing Teachers*. In a detailed section on evaluating student's writing assignments, Lindemann outlines excellent advice for any instructor facing a stack of student papers (pp. 216–219). She suggests the following procedure. First, read each student's paper through once without marking it. As you read, identify one or two major problems within the paper and formulate tentative hypotheses to explain the problems. Finally, examine what the student has done well. At this point, you are ready to make comments on the student's essay. Use questions to call attention to problems but avoid labelling problems unless you provide a way to solve them. Use praise to work toward improvements. Above all else, instructors should resist the temptation to rewrite the student's sentences—such rewriting suggests to students that they simply have written "in the way the instructor wants." Write a final comment that summarizes your comments and suggests a goal for the next assignment. Finally, keep track of the student's progress from assignment and/or as I always suggest, help the student formulate a way to keep track of her or his own progress.

Many instructors like to use forms for evaluation and construct point systems for recording a student's progress. The difficulty with such forms is that they almost inevitably lead to a system of checkmarks that may not finally provide with useful commentary. I favor writing comments on a student's paper and using letter grades that have been clearly defined, using pluses and minuses to indicate more refined assessments.

In addition to asking students to keep track of their progress on individual writing assignments throughout the semester, I provide a final grade evaluation sheet, which I share with students at the end of the semester. I have included an example of this form below. At a final conference with the student, I ask her or him to bring their own evaluation notes, and I give them this form (adaptable for different courses), filled out with my comments. I find it a good opportunity to discuss strengths and weaknesses with a student and make suggestions about what a student might do in the future to continue to progress and grow as a writer.

Introduction to College Writing—
Final Grade Evaluation

Student Name:

1. 5 short writing assignments—25 pages of revised, edited writing, all of which will include documentation of sources (45%)

   Assignment #1

   Assignment #2

   Assignment #3

   Assignment #4

   Assignment #5

   General Comments:

2. An oral presentation (10%)

   General Comments:

3. Announced and unannounced weekly in-class writing assignments, quizzes, and exercises (10%)

   General Comments:

4. Final Portfolio (includes two of the assignments above and a letter to me) (35%)

   General Comments:

Course Grade:

PORTFOLIOS

In general a portfolio is a collection of student writing which has been revised for presentation during a semester. The term is borrowed from art programs, where students often assemble a record of their best work to show to prospective employers. At many colleges and universities, portfolios of work in a variety of fields is encouraged and even required of students. In many writing programs, portfolios are a part of the final evaluation of a course. In some programs, students must submit a portfolio according to guidelines determined by the administrators and faculty members involved in the program; these portfolios may be evaluated in group grading sessions by faculty members. Often the portfolio assessment is a gateway to passing a course or writing proficiency requirement. But portfolios can serve other purposes as well. Many instructors use a portfolio as a way of having students collect their best work, revise it carefully, and submit it as a final writing assignment.

If you are teaching in a program or department that requires a portfolio, you and your students will doubtless have guidelines for the preparation and evaluation of the finished work. But if you are not, you may still wish to ask students to prepare a portfolio as a final assignment in the course. Decide how many assignments you want students to revise and present (I recommend two essays or writing assignments). Ask student to choose and revise these essays in consultation with you. A very effective summary assignment for the portfolio is to ask students to prepare a letter to accompany their folder of work. I use an assignment such as the following:

Introduction to College Writing

SELF-EVALUATION FOR YOUR PORTFOLIO

With your portfolio of two revised essay, you will write a cover letter in which you assess your work for this semester. Some questions that you should answer in this letter are:

1. Which of the revised papers in your portfolio represented the greatest challenge for you?
2. Which of your revised papers represents your best writing? What are the strengths of this paper? Is there anything now that you wish you had done differently?
3. How would you describe your improvement as a writer this semester? What have you learned that has been especially helpful? What resources have you learned to use that have helped you?
4. Which writing assignment did you enjoy the most? Why?

Asking students to prepare a letter based on their work in the course is an excellent way to have students conduct their own evaluations.

II

Section 1

LITERACY NARRATIVES

The selections in the opening section of the *Constructing Literacies* are narratives by a variety of writers describing how different people, in both formal and informal educational situations, achieved an awareness of the power of language, despite barriers of race, class, poverty, gender, physical impairment, and sometimes even physical danger.

The contemporary popularity of memoir and autobiography is such that most students will come to this section generally interested in life writing; for that reason, beginning the course with this section may work best in most classes. The term *literacy narrative,* however, may need some additional explanation. Each of the selections in this section was chosen for the way in which the writer discusses his or her experiences in acquiring language and the more complex skills of literacy within particular communities. Instructors might want to use the initial questions in the Introduction as a way of encouraging students to talk about their own experiences in achieving language and literacy.

1. MIKE ROSE

"I JUST WANNA BE AVERAGE"

from Lives on the Boundary *(New York: Penguin, 1989).*

When Mike Rose published *Lives on the Boundary* in 1989, he did not expect it to become a popular as well as a critical success. Widely reviewed in the scholarly and periodical press, *Lives on the Boundary* has become something of a classic of the literacy narrative genre. Rose's experiences in growing up in a working-class neighborhood in Los Angeles have captured the imaginations and attentions of students from New England to the Midwest to California. Most students will find this selection accessible and engaging.

Since Rose begins this chapter with a brief historical commentary on the wave of European immigration at the turn of the nineteenth and twentieth centuries, I often ask students in classes what they know about their own familial experiences. Asking students whose families were involved in this wave of immigration generally helps students (even those whose background is not European) understand the importance of this experience to a family. Students whose familial background is from other parts of the world can participate in the discussion by offering comparisons and contrasts. Rose's purpose in this chapter of *Lives on the Boundary* is to describe and explain the sometimes deadening and limiting effects of secondary schooling on children and adolescents. Asking students to comment on some of the passages in the text is an effective way to prompt discussion. For example, I always point out the lines: "Students will float to the mark you set. I and the others in the vocational classes were bobbing in pretty shallow water." Ask students to comment on these lines and what they know about such marks from their own school experiences. Rose describes his move out of the vocational track at Our Lady of Mercy, the devastating death of his father, and his consequent friendship with his gifted teacher, Jack MacFarland. At the end of the selection, Rose mentions a series of books he is reading and how these influence and change the direction of his life.

2. FREDERICK DOUGLASS

CHAPTER VII

from Narrative of the Life of Frederick Douglass, an American Slave, Written by Himself
(New York: Penguin, 1986).

Most students will be familiar with the story of the escaped slave, Frederick Douglass, since *The Narrative of the Life of Frederick Douglass* has recently become a part of the canon of antebellum American literature. Published as an anti-slavery tract by the Boston Anti-Slavery Society, the book was an important and popular tool of the abolitionists in their efforts to win support for the abolition of slavery. While students may be familiar with the general outlines of Douglass's story, they may not know, however, how Douglass's efforts to educate himself became such a crucial part of his escape from slavery. In this selection (Chapter VII of the *Narrative*), Douglass describes his life in Master Hugh's family in Baltimore, Maryland. Douglass explains the initial kindness of his mistress in helping him learn how to read and then his efforts to educate himself. Of particular interest in this section is Douglass's reading of *The Columbian Orator,* a collection of speeches, dialogues, and sermons from both ancient and contemporary sources. *The Columbian Orator* was a popular text in nineteenth-century schools designed to provide models for teaching young boys how to be effective public speakers and writers. (The text is now available in a contemporary edition, edited by David W. Blight for New York University Press in 1998). Instructors might encourage students to notice how Douglass comments on the lessons he learns from this text and he constructs his own lessons in literacy and language.

3. HELEN KELLER

"THE DAY LANGUAGE CAME INTO MY LIFE"

from The Story of My Life *(New York: Doubleday, 1905).*

A popular book that has not been out of print since its publication in 1905, Helen Keller's *The Story of My Life* will be familiar to virtually every student. Born in 1880 in Tuscumbia, Alabama, Helen Keller was born with normal hearing and sight but was stricken with a fever at eighteen months of age that left her deaf and blind. The inspirational story of her education by Anne Sullivan and her subsequent life has been the subject of movies and documentaries. The selection here is the fourth chapter of *The Story of My Life* in which Keller recounts her first understanding of what she calls the "mystery of language"—when she comprehends the connection between the symbols Sullivan used for the spelling of water and the splash of water on Keller's hand. This short selection with its memorable descriptions of the "dense fog" of Keller's life will be accessible to all students and serves as an effective illustration of the way in which one profoundly disabled woman achieved language and literacy.

4. ZITKALA-SA (GERTRUDE BONNIN)

"THE SCHOOL DAYS OF AN INDIAN GIRL"

Atlantic Monthly *(February 1900): 189–192.*

Zitkala-Sa was born Gertrude Simmons to a white father and a Dakota mother at the Yankton Sioux Agency in South Dakota may not be a familiar writer to most students. A frequent writer for the influential *Atlantic Monthly,* Zitkala-Sa shared space in this magazine with the likes of literary figures such as Mark Twain, Edith Wharton, Henry James, Hamlin Garland, and politicians such as Theodore Roosevelt, Grover Cleveland, and Woodrow Wilson. Like many Indian children at the end of the nineteenth century, Zitkala-Sa was sent to a missionary school for assimilation into white culture. Zitkala-Sa attended White's Manual Institute, a Quaker school in Indiana for six years. The selections printed in *Constructing Literacies* first appeared in the *Atlantic Monthly* in 1900. The selection opens with an account of how Zitkala-Sa was approached by missionaries from the White's Manual Institute. Students may want to discuss the title of the selection, "The Big Red Apples," and consider what promises are made to the children to attend the school. In the following parts of the this selection, Zitkala-Sa narrates her initial impressions of the school and the various ways in which the students are gradually acculturated into the ways of the white world. Of particular interest are the accounts of how the lessons Zitkala-Sa learns at the school are at odds with the native legends of her childhood. This selection ends with Zitkala-Sa at the beginning of her career as a student at Earlham College and a poignant account of the oratory contest she wins. The Questions for Reaction and Discussion and for Writing at the end of this selection invite students to consider contemporary marketing strategies used by colleges and universities as well as the significant difference between the literacy of Zitkala-Sa's native community and the literacy she learns at a white school and college.

5. MARY ANTIN

"INITIATION"

from The Promised Land *(Boston: Houghton Mifflin, 1912).*

Mary Antin was born a Jew in Czarist Russia at a time when Jews were a detested minority and being forced to emigrate to western Europe and the United States to avoid persecution. When Antin and her family arrived in Boston in 1894 to join her father who had gone to find work, they began the uphill struggle of learning to live in the United States. *The Promised Land,* published in 1901, was enormously successful, selling over eighty-five thousand copies sold in thirty-four printings. The success was due, in no small part, to Antin's enthusiasm for American life and for her optimistic tone and spirit. Students who are not familiar with the European immigrant experience at the turn of the nineteenth and twentieth centuries may be surprised by Antin's uncritical response to the United States and to her certainty that America was "the promised land."

The selections from *The Promised Land* printed in *Constructing Literacies* include two chapters, "The Promised Land" and "Initiation." The reading opens with Antin's arrival in the United States and her description of her father's efforts to find work. Antin described the situation of her father, a respected rabbi in Russia, who was unable to find comparable work in the United States. She also describes turn-of-the-century Boston and many fascinating details of her family's domestic life and arrangements, including an experience common to many immigrants: the alteration of her name into an American version. Most of the selection printed here, however, is devoted to Antin's narrative of her "intiation" into American education and her early experiences in school. She begins with a poignant account of the first days of school for Antin, her brother, and her sister. Included in her narrative of her early schooling is the reprinting of an essay, "Snow," Antin wrote that her teacher submitted it to a newspaper to demonstrate how quickly Antin had learned English. Instructors may want to point out the many passages in this selection that Antin discusses her early experiences in learning a new language and in writing. The reading ends with a description of Antin's promotion to grammar school. The Questions for Reaction and Discussion suggest some directions for classroom conversation about this selection. Instructors may wish to encourage students to discuss Antin's continual reference to the United States as a "garden" and to examine the implications of such a view.

6. ANDREA R. FISHMAN

"BECOMING LITERATE: A LESSON FROM THE AMISH"

from The Right to Literacy, *ed. Andrea A. Lunsford, Helene Moglen, and James Slevin*
(New York: MLA, 1990).

Fishman's essay on the Amish is the only selection in this section that is not, strictly speaking, a literacy narrative. A scholarly case study of Fishman's observations of an Old Order Amish family in Pennsylvania, this essay was originally a paper presented at the Right to Literacy Conference sponsored by the Modern Language Association in 1988. Fishman has studied the Amish extensively; with Glenda L. Bissex, she co-authored *Amish Literacy: What and How It Means* (1988). Instructors need not worry that students will not find this essay accessible; Fishman writes clearly and well. In her hands, the Fisher family becomes an intriguing group of people and not just a case study for analysis.

The essay begins with a description of the Fisher family on a Sunday evening and gives a clear sense of life for an Old Order Amish family. Fishman is careful to describe the important differences between what the Amish consider literacy and what most of mainstream American culture regards as literacy. Here, access to printed texts is carefully controlled by the parents and the collection of books and especially songbooks are all oriented toward what Fishman describes as "Amish-appropriate ways." Fishman clearly and carefully points such differences as the fact that critical reading, as taught and understood in mainstream schools, is considered divisive and is not valued by the Amish. Additionally, students in Old Order schools are not taught to value originality as desirable in writing. In every case, Fishman is careful to note what mainstream society "offers and what it takes away." She points out that Amish life rewards conformity to established norms. Fishman's purpose is to point out that there are many definitions of literacy and that some, like Old Order Amish, are at odds with what is taught in mainstream schools.

7. RICHARD RODRIGUEZ

"ARIA: A MEMOIR OF A BILINGUAL CHILDHOOD"

The American Scholar *50 (Winter 1980/81): 25–42.*

Richard Rodriguez, among the best-known Mexican American writers of today, may already be familiar to students for his essays in magazines and journals, as well as his frequent appearances on news programs. With impressive academic credentials and scholarships, Rodriguez seemed destined, in the 1960s, toward a career as an internationally-known professor. Instead, Rodriguez withdrew from his doctoral program at the University of California—Berkeley to write full-time. As a public intellectual, Rodriguez has taken controversial stands on such issues as affirmative action and bilingual education. "Aria," the selection reprinted here, first appeared in *The American Scholar,* the journal of Phi Beta Kappa.

In this selection, Rodriguez recounts his days as a Spanish-speaking student in a Roman Catholic elementary school in Sacramento, California. As he says, his understanding of English was limited to about fifty words. While the essay is autobiographical, Rodriguez uses his personal experiences to discuss his opposition to bilingual education and to explain how learning English changed his personal and public life. As a child, he regarded Spanish as a private, family language and English as a public language. In this essay, Rodriguez tracks the changes in his family as English became more of the language of home as well as the language of the public. Rodriguez ends his essay with a meditation on the connections between language and intimacy. The questions at the end of the reading offer suggestions to instructors and students about approaching this essay by discussing the nature of bilingual education and asking students to speculate on the many issues that writers like Rodriguez have raised.

8. MALCOLM X

"SAVED"

from The Autobiography of Malcolm X *(New York: Random House, 1964).*

Several of the authors of the selections in the first section of *Constructing Literacies* discuss the ways in which their names were changed or altered by achieving new literacies. Malcolm X was born Malcolm Little in Omaha, Nebraska. The son of a black man who supported African nationalism, Malcolm X left home at an early age and became involved in the urban world of New York City. Arrested for burglary in 1946, Malcolm X served a term in the Norfolk Prison Colony and later in the Charlestown State Prison. There he converted to Islam and after his release, he changed his name to Malcolm X. This chapter is from *The Autobiography of Malcolm X,* which was written with the assistance of Alex Haley, the author of *Roots.*

In this selection, "Saved," Malcolm X describes his conversion to Islam and his daily habit of writing to Elijah Muhammed and a variety of others, including his siblings and a variety of underworld figures that Malcolm X had known in Boston and New York. He explains that he became frustrated with his inability to convey all that he wanted in his letters and began a program of self-education by reading books in the Norfolk prison library. Malcolm X discusses his study of the dictionary and also his discovery of books on slavery. "Of course," he writes, "I read *Uncle Tom's Cabin.* " Throughout this selection, Malcolm X recounts what he learned from various books that he read and the impact they made on his thinking about himself, his African roots, his newfound religion, and his position in American society. As the Questions for Reaction and Discussion suggest, instructors might begin discussing this reading by inviting students to comment on Malcolm X's comparison of his homemade education with a college education.

9. LYDIA MINATOYA

"TRANSFORMATION"

from Talking to High Monks in the Snow *(New York: Harper Collins, 1992).*

Lydia Minatoya won the 1991 PEN/Jerard Fund Award for her autobiography, *Talking to High Monks in the Snow.* Born in Albany, New York to Japanese parents, Minatoya details the lives of her parents who were sent to a Wyoming internment camp for Japanese Americans in 1941. As in many of the selections in this sections of *Constructing Literacies,* this reading deals with the naming of the writer and the consequences of the name for the writer's future. Unlike Mary Antin, Lydia Minatoya possessed few illusions about the possibility for success for immigrants to the United States, and her book is filled with flat statements such as, "Call it denial, but many Japanese Americans never quite understood that the promise of America was not truly meant for them" or "And so my parents gave me an American name and hoped that I could pass. They nourished me with the American dream: Opportunity, Will, Transformation." Students may well need some explanation about Japanese internment camps; in the Questions for Further Explorations following the reading, some suggestions are given for sources of information about the camps and attitudes toward Japanese Americans after the bombing of Pearl Harbor.

In this reading, from the chapter entitled "Transformation," Minatoya begins with her recollections of her own childhood and her parents' experience in being escorted by armed guard to the Relocation Camps. Much of this reading is, however, devoted to a transformative experience that Minatoya has in an elementary school after her family has moved to the suburbs. Accustomed to being a "teacher's pet" in Albany, she recalls the taunts of white children in her new school and trying hard to replace a teacher's favorite student. The reading ends with Minatoya feigning sleep on the floor of a classroom. The experience, Minatoya, says broke a "spell."

10. GEORGE STEINER

"HERALDRY"

Granta *58 (1997): 147–57.*

In the final reading in this section, George Steiner, the distinguished literary and cultural critic, recounts his early childhood experience with a gift from an uncle—a pictorial guide to coats of arms in Salzburg and the surrounding area. This book made a lifelong impression on Steiner. The immediate context for Steiner's essay is the British literary magazine, *Granta,* which publishes the works of modern and contemporary writers. "Heraldry" appeared in a special issue with the theme of "Ambition." The historical context for this selection is Europe in the 1930s and the events leading to the catastrophic Holocaust to come.

Steiner describes in considerable detail what this pictoral guide taught him about diversity, as he says, "the diversity of human purposes, artifacts, representations or concealments" and later, "a fathomless depth of differentiation, of non-identity, always incipient with the eventuality of chaos." Steiner then recalls the early details of his childhood in Paris, where his parents had moved after the climate of Vienna was thought to be too harsh for his father's "rheumatic fevers." Steiner's father also feared the rising tide of anti-Jewish sentiment in Austria. His father, a brilliant investment banker, was also a writer and passionately interested in his son's education. Much of the essay concerns the many lessons that Steiner's father taught him. It is an account of a remarkable education, a "totally trilingual" upbringing against a "polyglot" backdrop. The Questions for Reaction and Discussion at the end of the reading suggest that instructors may encourage students to tackle this essay by considering the relationship between the pictorial guide to coats and arms and the process of Steiner's education under the direction of his father.

USING THE SUGGESTIONS FOR FURTHER READING, THINKING, AND WRITING TO DESIGN WRITING ASSIGNMENTS FOR SECTION 1

A variety of suggestions are given in the Questions for Writing at the end of each reading, and instructors may want to consider using some of these as short, preliminary assignments in preparation for a longer essay. For example, many of the selections deal, at least in part, with the effect of teachers on the literacy acquisition of the writers. Asking students to write brief accounts of teachers in two or three of the selections (such as the narratives of Helen Keller, Lydia Minatoya, and Mike Rose) will provide some preliminary material for a longer essay on teachers. In the Suggestions for Further Reading, Thinking, and Writing, assignment 3 calls for an essay on effective teaching based on the readings in this section.

If an instructor feels that beginning a course with an assignment based more firmly on a student's personal experience is an effective way to begin, I suggest which assignment 10 invites a student to write his or her own literacy narrative.

One way to encourage group activity in a writing assignment is to take an assignment such as 6 and work with the class to develop a questionnaire about the variety of experiences the students have had in their educational lives to this point. Students can then participate in the survey, assemble the results, and work in groups to write a report of sections of the questionnaire. Such collaborative assignments in the early part of a course can help build a class's confidence in one another and can also serve to help the students get to know one another better.

Instructors who wish to introduce some research and use of outside sources immediately might consider assignments 1, 4, or 7 which could be used to ask students to read other sources and locate other literacy narratives. Basil Johnston's experiences, for example, in a Canadian school for Indian children, might provide a male perspective on the similar experiences of Zitkala-Sa.

Finally, asking students to use two or three of the selections in this section is a good way to introduce them to the process of handling differing views and perspectives on a similar topic. Making comparisons and contrasts and thinking through the implications in an assignment that calls for some consideration of more than one of the readings can help students move into more complex forms of writing assignments.

The following assignment, Writing Project 1, is a suggestion for this section of *Constructing Literacies*.

SAMPLE WRITING ASSIGNMENT

Writing Assignment 1

Topic

Classification and comparison/contrast of literacy/socialization narratives.

Reading Required

Assigned narratives from Section 1 of your textbook.

Length of Completed Essay

4–5 pages

Format/Documentation Style

MLA

Deadlines

Personal narrative and group work: Week 2
Essay outline and draft due for peer edit and discussion: Week 3
Revised essay due: Week 4

Step-by-Step Instructions

1. Read the assigned narratives and participate in class discussion about them.
2. In class, write a brief, informal literacy narrative of your own.
3. In your in-class writing group, read and discuss one another's narratives and classify them as "socialization narratives" or "literacy narratives" using the category explanations in

Suggestions for Further Reading, Thinking, and Writing. Look at the narratives you are reading for class and find two of them that fit into the same category as your personal narrative.

4. On your own, reread the two narratives carefully, take notes, and think about how the two narratives resemble/differ from each other and your personal narrative.

5. Make a list of similarities and differences and then construct an outline showing the most significant similarities and differences, making sure to show how they fit into the "literacy" or "socialization" category.

6. Draft an essay in which you compare and contrast the professionally written narratives to your own and discuss how they all qualify as "socialization" or "literacy" narratives. Be sure that your essay has a strong thesis statement tying all the points together and that your ideas are organized clearly.

7. Bring the draft to class for peer edit and discussion. Each writing group will critique its members' drafts and make suggestions for improvement. We will then have a full-class discussion about the results of the peer-editing session. After the discussion, submit the draft and peer-edit sheet for the instructor's review.

8. After reviewing the comments and suggestions of your classmates and instructor, revise, edit, and proofread the draft. Review the evaluation criteria on the syllabus and this assignment sheet to make sure that you have met all the requirements of the assignment. Submit your revised essay to the instructor for evaluation. To revise your draft, first resolve content and organizational problems, then move on to paragraphing and transitions, sentence structure, word choice, clarity, etc. Then edit to correct problems with grammar and usage, style, punctuation, mechanics, format, etc. Use your spell-checker and correct any problems that it finds and then proofread the essay yourself to find any typographical errors or other problems that the spell-checker did not catch.

Section 2

THE PURPOSE OF A COLLEGE EDUCATION

In this section of *Constructing Literacies,* a variety of writers offer opinions about the set of skills and knowledge students should learn in college and what the general purposes of an education should be. In a departure from the use of mainly contemporary sources throughout *Constructing Literacies,* this section begins with a fascinating excerpt from a faculty committee report at Yale in 1828. Students will be surprised at how familiar the arguments may sound.

As I say in the Introduction to this section, Americans in general share the view that a college education is important if not crucial to an adult. But what the nature and purpose of that education should be remains debatable, as the essays and articles in this section show. Instructors may want to open the discussion of the readings in this section by asking students some of the questions that are listed in the Introduction, such as what they know about the history of higher education and what a "liberal arts" education means. Students might also want to talk about what they expect to learn in the course of their college educations. Instructors might wish to make notes of what the students say (or ask them to make notes) and examine these notes periodically during the course of reading and studying the selections in this section.

1. COMMITTEE OF THE CORPORATION AND ACADEMICAL FACULTY

from Reports on the Course of Instruction in Yale College
(New Haven: Hezekiah Howe, 1828).

This excerpt from this fascinating faculty committee report makes for interesting reading, even in the twenty-first century. Instructors will recognize the language of a committee as the author of the report, and students may be surprised to see how detailed the report is. As the headnote for this selection explains, the immediate context for the report was a request (primarily from students and alumni) to consider altering what was then the "regular course of instruction" of the college, which required all students to study Latin and

Greek. The request asked the college to considering substituting other, more contemporary fields and studies in place of the courses in Latin and Greek. Since the study of classical languages was a primary part of the curriculum at Yale (and indeed at other colleges at this time), altering the curriculum was a major undertaking. The two-part report that is excerpted here includes a summary of the "plan of education in the college" and an assessment of the value of the study of classical languages.

The first part of the report begins with the admission of the faculty committee that the "present plan of education admits of improvement." But the faculty members quickly defend the curriculum by pointing out the number of changes that have been made, such as the introduction of a series of new disciplines with courses in chemistry, mineralogy, geology, and political economy. The report then explains that it is not possible to determine whether the curriculum should be changed without first discussing what the object of higher education should be. The faculty members agree that the purpose is to "lay the foundation of a superior education" for a student body that still requires a "substitute for parental superintendence." To that end, the faculty committee suggests that intellectual culture is gained through the cultivation of "discipline and the furniture of the mind," which they define as "expanding" the powers of the mind and "storing" it with knowledge. Discipline is, however, of more importance in a college education. The committee report discusses the implications of these points and also the importance of providing a "substitute for parental superintendence." Contemporary college students, especially in institutions were there are large number of nontraditional students, may find this a curious matter for the attention of a faculty curriculum committee. Of particular importance in this part of the report is the fact that the committee excludes "professional studies" from the responsibility of those charged with providing undergraduate education. Instructors may wish to encourage students to examine the mission statements of their own institutions and even assign them as supplementary reading, as the Questions for Writing at the end of the reading suggest.

2 .   R I C H A R D   H .   H E R S H

"INTENTIONS AND PERCEPTIONS: A NATIONAL SURVEY OF PUBLIC ATTITUDES TOWARD LIBERAL ARTS EDUCATION"

Change (March/April 1997), pp. 16–22.

With the support of the AT&T Foundation, Richard H. Hersh, the President of Hobart and William Smith Colleges, commissioned a national survey to investigate attitudes toward liberal arts programs within universities and colleges entirely devoted to the liberal arts. A good way to begin the discussion of this reading is to make sure that students understand the various kinds of institutions—even such basics as the difference between a liberal arts college and a research-oriented university. The purpose of Hersh's study is to clarify attitudes of contemporary Americans about the liberal arts. As such, the report of Hersh's study is a valuable document for the study of the meaning and value of a liberal arts education, as perceived by a series of respondent groups. Instructors might encourage students to consider carefully how they would have responded to the questions on the survey and to the twelve findings that Hersh reports in this reading.

Since this reading is in the form of a report and not an essay, some students may need assistance in reading the charts and following the discussion. In general, Hersh clearly labels the statistics that support the twelve findings, which are:

- Few people still believe in the importance of learning for learning's sake.
- Parents and high school students have little or no idea what a liberal arts education is.
- Other than faculty members and liberal arts college graduates, few groups have positive feelings toward liberal arts education.
- Most people believe you can get a liberal arts education anywhere—it's not unique.
- On a number of measures, business executives have greater faith in the effectiveness of a liberal arts education than do parents.
- Students and parents believe that the reason to go to college is to prepare for a degree, but fewer than 40 percent of business executives agree.
- Most people agree that problem-solving, critical thinking, and writing and oral skills are career skills and are the most important goals of higher education.
- Liberal arts colleges should teach skills for the workplace.
- No college or university is performing well, according to business executives, except small liberal arts colleges in culture/arts appreciation and foreign language teaching.
- More than one-third of parents consider liberal arts education a luxury beyond their reach.
- Belief in the importance of a college education is significantly lower among college and high school faculty and administrators than in society at large.
- Most people believe students at all types of institutions party too much.

Anyone of Hersh's findings will help set the stage for provocative discussions with students, but instructors might especially stress the differences between the attitudes of business executives and students and their parents.

3 . WAYNE C. BOOTH

"IS THERE ANY KNOWLEDGE THAT A MAN MUST HAVE?"

from The Knowledge Most Worth Having *(Chicago: University of Chicago Press, 1967)*.

3 . WAYNE C. BOOTH

"IS THERE ANY KNOWLEDGE THAT A WOMAN MUST HAVE?"

from The Vocation of a Teacher *(Chicago: University of Chicago Press, 1988)*.

These readings are grouped together in *Constructing Literacies* for a couple of reasons. First, the essays are companion pieces. After Wayne Booth developed the speech that was later developed into the published essay that was published in 1967, he began to have complaints from women who felt excluded from his essay by the use of *man* in the title and the emphasis on masculine pronouns throughout. Instructors might note for their students that it was when the essay was anthologized in a text frequently used in first-year writing courses, *The Norton Anthology of Expository Prose,* that Booth began to receive comments from students and instructors using the book. Booth has said about this experience that he wrote this essay before the feminist critique of language was underway and that he was a writer who needed that critique. The second essay, first delivered as a talk in 1980, is a meditation on the first essay and a discussion of what Booth learned in the process. Another reason to include both essays together is to demonstrate some revision practices to students. In the second essay, Booth talks a good bit about revising his opinions and also comments directly on many of the ideas and concepts in his first essay. Instructors might want to take the opportunity of using this pair of essays to focus on the notion of revision in their discussions.

In "Is There Any Knowledge That a Man Must Have?, Booth begins with a discussion of how we "all get along without vast loads of learning" and establishes his discussion on the basis of what a liberal arts education ought to offer a "man" in order to be fully human. Booth surveys and explains three historical notions of what knowledge a "man" needs and how to education him: as a complex machine that needs to be programmed; as an animal with a collection of drives that can be conditioned to learn; and a members of a group that must learn to function as units in society. These portraits of what a man is are inappropriate, metaphorical definitions of man to Booth, and he spends the second part of this essay explaining the complications of defining men in metaphorical terms. Booth explains that a liberal education is suited to men because "it is intended to liberate men from whatever it is that makes animals act like animals and machines act like machines." To Booth, a liberal education teaches a man to learn for himself, which first involves knowing something about how own nature and his place in "Nature" and being able to think critically and test speculations. Second, Booth explains that a man must be educated in the experience of beauty and know how to "make the great human achievements in the arts his own;" and finally, a man must know how "to understand his own intentions and to make them effective in the world." Booth concludes the essay by suggesting that colleges have a responsibility to teach a man how to use his mind in the three directions he has outlined.

The second essay, "Is There any Knowledge That a Woman Must Have?" begins with a recital of the events under which "Is There Any Knowledge that a Man Must Have?" was written and presented. Booth explains that he was surprised by the letters he received about his essay, but only when he reread it did he realize how "male-centered" it was. Booth was shocked, he explains, to realize that although he thought of himself as an enlightened man, the language of his first essay suggested otherwise. Acting on the premise that he can simply revise the essay by substituting "people," "students," or "human beings" for "men," Booth is further startled to realize that he has in fact made some statements that do not translate easily. Not wishing to deal with the question of whether men and women are essentially different, Booth chooses to write the essay about an additional task for women: how to cope with men and review the difficulties of his first essay that are not simply about simple substitutions in words. Booth reviews a variety of examples from popular culture, commenting on messages that are sent about women to men—the number of representations of women as objects. Booth wonders what kind of education women need to cope with those images and the training that culture provides men. He ends his essay with "four neglected liberal arts that every woman must master": the art of strategy, the art of persuasion, the criticism of metaphors for human life and for the self, and the criticism of situations or circumstances. Booth conceives of the first two arts as arts of winning and the second two as arts of reconstitution.

Taken together, these essays form a fascinating reflection on the power of language and metaphor to shape the way in which we view ourselves and our educations. The Questions for Reaction and Discussion following the end of the second essay are intended to encourage students to read and examine these essays together. The Questions for Writing suggest similar ways to think of the essays together, but also provide ideas for writing assignments for one or the other essay.

5 . MARK EDMUNDSON

"ON THE USES OF A LIBERAL EDUCATION: I. AS LITE ENTERTAINMENT FOR BORED COLLEGE STUDENTS"

Harper's Magazine *(September 1997), pp. 39–49.*

The headnote for this selection point out that many of the readings in this second section of *Constructing Literacies* are concerned with the college curriculum and how it promotes or does not promote a liberal education. Mark Edmundson, a professor of English at the University of Virginia, chooses to discuss the culture of the contemporary college campus to examine what the culture suggests about the current state of a liberal education.

Edmundson begins anecdotally, detailing a scenario that will be all-too-familiar to instructors: student evaluation day. From a brief meditation on the implications for him as a teacher, Edmundson explains his position: the goals and purposes of a traditional liberal arts education is that college culture, like American culture, is "ever more devoted to consumption and entertainment, to the using and using up of goods and images." Edmundson's thesis is that instead of examining the curriculum, those who are in search of the state of liberal education in the United States should turn their attention to the culture of classrooms and campuses. The essay is, in many ways, an excellent example of a cultural critique. It is also witty and reflective with a good many memorable lines. Instructors at primarily residential colleges and universities will identify with Edmundson's statement, "Over the past few years, the physical layout of my university has been changing. To put it a little indecorously, the place is looking more and more like a retirement spread for the young."

Edmundson skillfully analyzes the culture of television as Marshall McCluhan's "cool medium" and analyzes the absence of strong emotions on a campus. The cool youth culture is low-key and nonassertive. Edmundson analyzes the pervasive consumer mentality of students; he does not blame them, he is quick to say, and offers an analysis of the social and cultural forces that have led to this state. He analyzes the ways in which universities solicit students and the tone of the materials sent to perspective students. He takes up the question of what "decentered" classrooms mean and whose authority counts (it is seldom the professor). Edmundson's conclusion is that the consumer ethos is winning at contemporary universities. Edmundson concludes his essay with a call for celebrating individualism, for praising genius, and for enthusiasm. Instructors and students will find many provocative statements and passages in this essay; students will undoubtedly want to challenge Edmundson's critique of their culture. The Questions for Reaction and Discussion suggest some ways to direct such discussions.

6 .   M A R T H A   C .   N U S S B A U M

"THE OLD EDUCATION AND THE THINK-ACADEMY"

from Cultivating Humanity: A Classical Defense of Reform in Liberal Education
(Cambridge: Harvard University Press, 1997).

Strongly interested in how students can develop global perspectives within American colleges and universities, Martha C. Nussbaum, a professor of philosophy and law, spent a couple of years visiting colleges and universities to study how institutions are meeting the challenge of increasing cultural diversity on their campuses. In this chapter from the book that emerged from her study, *Cultivating Humanity: A Classical Defense of Reform in Liberal Education,* Nussbaum contrasts what she has observed and studied on American campuses with what is often reported in the popular press. Drawing on her extensive knowledge of classical literature, Nussbaum deftly introduces Socrates as an educational radical. In the Questions for Reading, I suggest that students recall what they know about Greek drama and Socrates; instructors might wish to make a specific assignment to students about finding information if a particular group of students seems to have limited experience with classical literature.

Nussbaum uses the example of Aristophanes' *The Clouds* to stress the historical nature of our contemporary arguments on the nature of education. Socrates is the radical figure—the representative of the "New Education" of the "Think-Academy," which stresses critical thinking and questioning of authority. Nussbaum suggests that current debates about higher education mirror the debate in *The Clouds* between the "Old" and "New Education." Nussbaum's purpose is to reveal the "real story of higher education in America" and the actuality of what is occurring on a variety of college campuses.

Rather than the usual focus on two or three well-known institutions, Nussbaum visited several different kinds of institutions, stressing how the press has concentrated its attention on a very small number of colleges. Instead of visiting Dartmouth, for example, Nussbaum visits St. Lawrence University; instead of the University of Michigan, she visits the University of Nevada. Instructors might want to spend a few minutes talking with students about the significance of the choices Nussbaum has made in her visits. Throughout this reading, Nussbaum presents interviews with students and faculty members and accounts of her actual conversations.

From her research, Nussbaum has concluded that for the most part, "We are now trying to build an academy in which women, and members of religious and ethnic minorities, and lesbian and gay people, and people living in non-Western cultures can be seen and also heard, with respect and love, both as knowers and as object of study, an academy in which to be a 'fellowess' need not mean being called 'courtesan' an academy in which the world will be seen to have many types of citizens and in which we can all learn to function

as citizens of that entire world." To Nussbaum, the purpose of a liberal education—the cultivation of humanity—is to produce good citizens. She sees
three capacities as essential to the cultivation of humanity:

- The capacity for critical examination of oneself and one's traditions.
- The capacity to see themselves not simply as citizens of some local
  region or group but also as human beings of an international world.
- The capacity for "narrative imagination," the ability to understand the
  emotions, needs, and desires of a person different from one's self.

These capacities are the departure points for Nussbaum's definition of intelli-
gent citizenship. Nussbaum concludes her essay by revisiting the examples of
the campuses she has visited and pointing out how the capacities for cultivating humanity have been integrated into the college curriculum.

One of the most teachable aspects of this essay is Nussbaum's presentation of Eric Chalmers, the student at Nevada who is resistant to courses that
seem to "teach" views that are not consistent with his own. Several of the
Questions for Reaction and Discussion and for Writing are designed to help
instructors engage students in discussions about how contemporary colleges
and universities are training students in the cultivation of humanity. Instructors may wish to encourage students to discuss their own experience with
resistance and how they have or are in the process of overcoming it.

7. DENISE K. MAGNER

"PROFESSORS AND INFLUENTIAL ALUMNI JOIN FORCES TO PROTECT BROOKLYN COLLEGE'S CORE CURRICULUM"

The Chronicle of Higher Education *(October 17, 1997), pp. A12–15.*

One of the purposes of including this essay in this section of *Constructing Literacies* is to help students understand how controversial general education or
core curriculum requirements can be on a college campus. Students may need
some assistance in understanding what these terms mean and also who decides
such requirements on a campus. One of the Questions for Reading suggests
that students learn what the requirements are in their own institution; instructors may wish to assign a few pages in the college catalogue or direct students
to the college Web site as a preliminary reading assignment for this essay. In
any case, instructors may well wish to begin discussion of this reading by asking about what the students understand their requirements to be and what
they know of the rationale for them.

This article is an account of how a proposal to transform the core curriculum at Brooklyn College was derailed by faculty opposition, the interven-
tion of an active alumni group, and negative publicity about the proposed
changes. The Brooklyn Core Curriculum, in place since 1981, requires all students to complete ten courses, which are listed at the end of the reading. Traditional departments at Brooklyn—such as philosophy, history, and
English—offer sections of these courses. Called "Brooklyn Connections," the
proposal to alter the curriculum involved restructuring these courses according
to four broad themes: Community Studies, Communications, Environmental
Studies, and Science Education. According to Denise Magner, the author of this
article, faculty members were concerned about these new themes would alter
the traditional nature of the courses in the curriculum and how they would
affect appointments to traditional academic departments. As several administrators that Magner interviewed pointed out, the controversy at Brooklyn
began to mirror national concerns over the liberal arts in higher education.

As the Questions for Writing indicate, instructors may wish to ask students to use this article as a springboard to examining the core curriculum at
their own institutions as well as investigating course descriptions of the Brooklyn Core. Students may wonder about the tensions that exist among faculty
members about core requirements; instructors might encourage students to
examine their own feelings about required courses as a way of thinking about
how and why college faculties put requirements in place. Instructors interested in incorporating group work into their classes may take the opportunity to
place students in teams to investigate the core requirements at several institutions and present papers on their findings during an in-class conference on
general education requirements.

8 .   G E O R G E   R .   H O U S T O N ,   J R .

"BURY THE LIBERAL VS. PROFESSIONAL ARTS DEBATE"

Education 117 (1996): 12–17.

For many students and their families, the tensions between education designed
for a liberal education and education designed for professional training are
real and problematic. If instructors have assigned the Committee of the Corporation and Academical Faculty from Reports on the Course of Instruction
in Yale College at the beginning of this section, they may wish to remind students of how firmly the Yale faculty committee rejects the notion that a college education involves professional training of any kind. With the enormous
number of programs in business, law, and medicine at American colleges and
universities, such divisions in the curriculum may strike many students as
being irrelevant. However, in the minds of many faculty members, the purpose
of a college education remains centrally about training in the liberal arts. In

this essay, written by the President of Mount Saint Mary's College, the argument suggests that the divide between liberal arts and the professional arts is a false one and should be abandoned. The Questions for Reading invite students to assess the tension between the liberal arts and professional training on their own campuses as a way to think about the issues that Houston raises.

Houston begins the essay with an historical survey of the debate, citing John Henry Newman's *The Idea of University* (1852) and Alfred North Whitehead's *The Aims of Education and Other Essays* (1929). Both Newman and Whitehead agree that a liberal education is crucial, and Houston urges that the views of the two can be combined for a sound program in higher education today. He comments that the best preparation for any profession or vocation is a sound liberal arts education that includes three general areas of knowledge: "Understanding of historical events and of different cultures; interaction with diverse groups on various intellectual levels; and appreciation of global economic, political and social forces present in the world today." To Houston, there is no necessary distinction between the professional and liberal arts in the aquisition of a "general culture of mind."

Using the example of a seminar taught at Mount Saint Mary's College, Houston explains that courses can be designed that promote theory and practice quite effectively. He concludes his essay by suggesting that the "best of the academic houses" are crafting missions that "will include not only an 'education for life' but an education that provides the skills, wisdom, and knowledge to get employed."

The Questions for Writing invite students to consider this essay in several ways. Students may be encouraged to investigate Newman and Whitehead, Houston's primary sources for this essay and consider how these views of education shape or don't shape the missions of their own colleges. Instructors may wish to use the Houston essay as a way of inviting comparisons with other essays. How, for instance, does this essay compare with that of Edmundson? To introduce some oral presentations in a class, instructors might consider assigning a pair of students to individual essays and staging a mock debate (in the style of recent political debates) over a series of questions about the purposes of a college education.

9. LISA SCHMEISER

"DO GEEKS NEED TO GO TO COLLEGE?"

Salon Magazine *(April 12, 1999).*
http://www.salonmagazine.com/tech/feature/1999/04/12/college/index.html

One of the intriguing aspects of this essay is that although it appears in print form in *Constructing Literacies,* this essay was written for *Salon,* the internet magazine. One of the Questions for Reading directs students to this fact about the essay; instructors may wish to encourage students students to think about the difference between reading an essay on a page and reading one on a screen. In addition, the essay specifically addresses the kind of education and training people need to have in order to be successful in fields involving emerging technologies and electronic culture. Students may be interested in learning more about Lisa Schmeiser herself, who is a former biology major and today is a successful writer and Web site developer.

Schmeiser begins with an arresting anecdote about Brad Ink, a former interior design major turned "information architect" who thinks in terms of the "critical adjacencies of space" on Web sites. Reminding her readers of the burgeoning job opportunities of the Web industry, Schmeiser speaks frankly about the high number of people who are trading a college education for an immediate high-paying job. Not only has this phenomenon affected undergraduate education, of course, there has been a recent impact on business programs and schools. And Schmeiser points to a high profile college dropout: Bill Gates. Steven Jobs, the head of Macintosh Computers, is also a college dropout.

But Schmeiser's article is actually an affirmative answer to the question of her title, "Do Geeks Need to Go to College?" Analyzing the results of an extensive online argument hosted by *Slashdot,* Schmeiser suggests that most Web designers and producers feel that their nontechnical degrees have provided them with important skills in communication, innovation, flexibility, and problem-solving. Schmeiser's conclusion, comforting to instructors, is that a college education is indeed useful to a person contemplating a highly technical job in an electronic culture.

At the end of the article, Schmeiser suggests that colleges might want to do more in thinking about what degrees provide the best training in the kinds of flexible thinking she deems as necessary to successful careers. Instructors might begin the discussion of this reading by asking how many students expect to go into a career involving the Internet and computers. From there, students might wish to discuss the particular skills they think they need and how they think the courses they are currently taking will help develop those. Instructors who wish to incorporate some interviewing techniques into their syllabi might consider inviting a Web developer or two to visit the class and have the class prepared to ask questions about the developer's background and training.

USING THE SUGGESTIONS FOR FURTHER READING, THINKING, AND WRITING TO DESIGN WRITING ASSIGNMENTS FOR SECTION 2

The variety of essays in this section lend themselves to several comparison and contrast writing assignments. In Questions 1 and 8, for example, students are asked to contrast the views they have read and show how the views differ. This is an especially useful exercise for students who have difficulty in discriminating different points of view. Instructors who feel that their students need additional work in this area might try Question 8 which asks students to "interview" Mark Edmundson and Martha Nussbaum and prepare responses for how they think these two writers would respond.

Actively involving students in the debate of the purpose of a college education can often be accomplished by asking students to draw up their own survey instruments. In Question 7, students are asked to construct a questionnaire designed to find out the reasons why friends and classmates are attending college. In this assignment, students become researchers and must summarize and analyze their own results.

Other writing assignments suggested here involve asking students to investigate the history of their own institutions and do some additional reading and studying about the purpose of higher education. In my experience, students frequently respond well to assignments that ask them to present their views for a student audience—the college newspaper or a student page the professor might establish on his or her Web site. The purpose of this section of *Constructing Literacies* is to provide some of the background information and central arguments in the debate about the purpose of college. "Publishing" student responses is a very effective way of illustrating that first-year students have a right to participate in that debate.

SAMPLE WRITING ASSIGNMENT

Writing Assignment 2— What's a College Education For?

Read

Booth, Edumndson, Houston, and Nussbaum.

Consider

All of the essays above either challenge or defend what is best for a student to learn in college. Your task now is to think critically and carefully about your own educational goals in light of the institutional goals that are public information at your college or university and the goals that the academics you've read have outlined. In this assignment, you will write a persuasive essay about what you think are appropriate general education requirements for yourself.

continued

Plan

Your task is to write an essay in which you outline the goals of a liberal arts education for yourself and defend those goals in a carefully defined argument. Begin by thinking about the formal goals that institutions use and then make your own list. It might be helpful to think of this essay as a defense of why you are attending college (especially in light of the essays you read to prepare for this topic). Think of the members of our class as your audience—what evidence can you use to persuade them to accept your view?

Use the information you learned about your own and other schools and feel free to cite the sources that you read in our text. You will also want to do some additional reading, and by now, you should be familiar with the way to find essays, articles, books, and other resources in the library and on the Internet.

Research

You will need to use a minimum of three outside sources in your essay, one of which should be a printed source that you locate in our library and one of which should be an Internet resource.

Write and Rewrite

Write a draft of you essay. Revise carefully, taking into consideration comments and suggestions that I have made on earlier essays.

Edit

Make sure that each resource you mention is prepared in correct MLA form and that you include a list of Works Cited at the end of your essay.

Schedule

- October 20—Discuss assignment and essays.
- October 22—Workshop session on essay.
- October 27—Drafts due in class; peer evaluation.
- October 29—Writing Assignment #2 due in class; self-evaluation.

Section 3

LITERACIES FOR A DIVERSE WORLD

Perhaps the single most important challenge faced by colleges and universities in recent years has been responding to the increasing diversity of the student population of the United States. As the Introduction to this section suggests, E. D. Hirsch was among the first to raise this issue as a topic of major concern when he published his book *Cultural Literacy*, which became a national bestseller. Hirsch maintained that despite the cultural pluralism of American society, education (especially elementary and secondary education) should focus on common cultural information, "core knowledge" as Hirsch defines it. Consequently, the key to Hirsch's definition of literacy is information; and an "Appendix List" of terms was important supplement to *Cultural Literacy*. When the *New York Times Book Review* reviewed the book in 1987, it included some terms from the list in a box designed as a quiz for the culturally literate. Today, the term *cultural literacy* has largely been replaced by *multicultural literacy*, and the question today is how colleges and universities can more effectively promote the relationship between a culturally diverse society and the curriculum.

Instructors might begin a general discussion of the readings in this section by inviting responses to the initial quotation from bell hooks's *Talking Back*, "Education as the practice of freedom [is] not a force which fragments or separates, but one that brings us closer, expanding our definitions of home and community." Asking students how they think their educations to date have fragmented or expanded their notions of "home and community" will provide opportunities for students to discuss the issues that are at stake in curricular discussions. All but one of the selections in this section are written by professors; students might also consider how teaching methods (especially those they have experienced in the past) reflect various philosophies of education. Finally, this section is a good one to remind students about the various ways in which groups resist cultural pluralism. Ask students to recall how Mike Rose, Mary Antin, or Richard Rodriguez responded to their "difference" in the societies in which they found themselves. Finally, an effective pre-writing activity for this section is to invite student to write a definition of *multiculturalism* and discuss with their classmates the positive and negative charges that term has developed in contemporary usage.

1 .   E .   D .   H I R S C H

"Literacy and Cultural Literacy" and "The Appendix List"

from Cultural Literacy *(New York: Vintage, 1988).*

This section begins with E. D. Hirsch's introduction to his best-selling book, *Cultural Literacy.* In this book, Hirsch famously defines cultural literacy as the possession of "the basic information needed to thrive in the modern world." The emphasis on information—and on a core of information—set the stage for a debate that had a profound effect on the curricular discussions of the 1990s on college campuses across the country. The list of terms at the end of the selection is taken from the Appendix List of *Cultural Literacy* and was intended by Hirsch and the co-authors of his list to be guidelines for constructing such lists. Inevitably, however, the list became a very controversial part of *Cultural Literacy* and many of the reviewers of the book took great satisfaction in pointing out omissions or apparently odd choices.

The reason that the list was important to Hirsch was as a general illustration of his major thesis that national literacy depends on all citizens possessing a core knowledge base. To Hirsch, the past emphasis on skills in elementary and secondary schools has devalued the importance of teaching information to students. Cultural literacy depends, according to Hirsch, on "large amounts of specific information," shared by a large number of people. Hirsch emphasizes his point by providing a series of examples from his own experience and from standardized tests designed to measure students abilities to understand written materials, such as the National Assessment of Educational Progress (NAEP) mandated by Congress. One of Hirsch's striking examples is his discussion of an experiment he conducted in Richmond, Virginia in which most seventeen- and eighteen-year-olds were unable to place the Civil War in the second half of the nineteenth century and could not identify Ulysses S. Grant and Robert E. Lee. A second example, and one that Hirsch discusses at some length, is the use of the phrase, "There is a tide" taken from a passage in *Julius Caesar.* The failure of large numbers of people to recognize the allusion suggests to Hirsch that the background knowledge that we have in common is dwindling. Eventually Hirsch feels that the gap will widen so far as to cause severe economic, social, civic, and educational implications. As Hirsch strongly states, "To be truly literate, citizens must be able to grasp the meaning of any piece of writing addressed to the general reader. All citizens should be able, for instance, to read newspapers of substance. . . ."

Stressing the importance of the common knowledge necessary to "decode" general texts, Hirsch then discusses the importance of being able to grasp the "general shape of what we are reading and to tie it to what we already know." Hirsch explains that the ability to grasp the "general shape" depends on fairly superficial knowledge. Hirsch feels that schools have failed to teach cultural literacy because of the enormously influential "content neutral" educational theories of Rousseau and Dewey, which have promoted the skills of critical thinking in the schools. Additionally, Hirsch deplores the fragmentation that is the natural result of the sixteen thousand separate school districts that govern American elementary and secondary schools. Defending mainstream culture from the charge that it is generally a conservative culture, Hirsch cites the work of Orlando Patterson who points out that mainstream culture is constantly changing and assimilating new ideas and patters. Finally, Hirsch devotes the last part of this essay to a discussion of the importance of early schooling in cultural literacy, observing, "To thrive, a child needs to learn the traditions of the particular human society and culture it is born into."

Students will enjoy paging through the section of the Appendix List that follows the reading selection. An effective way to generate discussion is to ask students to quiz themselves on the terms and determine whether they have what Hirsch terms enough superficial knowledge to understand the terms given. In the Questions for Writing, instructors are encouraged to invite consideration of what it means to construct a *list* and asked to consider the effectiveness (and the limitations) of lists. Students might also enjoy visiting Hirsch's Core Knowledge Foundation Web site http://www.coreknowledge.org and investigating the extent to which Hirsch has built an entire elementary school curriculum on his ideas.

2. RICK SIMONSON AND SCOTT WALKER

"INTRODUCTION AND OPENING THE AMERICAN MIND: A PRELIMINARY LIST"

from Multicultural Literacy *(St. Paul: Graywolf Press, 1988).*

Among the many responses to the publication of Hirsch's *Cultural Literacy* was *Multicultural Literacy,* a collection of readings compiled by two professional publishers for specific use in college and university courses. Designed to counter *Cultural Literacy,* Simonson and Walker assembled the works of a variety of writers from diverse backgrounds, including James Baldwin, Paula Gunn Allen, Carlos Fuentes, David Mrua, Gloria Anzaldua, and Ishmael Reed. In addition to the readings, Simonson and Walker compiled their own list of terms for an Appendix List, in an effort not so much to construct a list of terms everyone should know but to demonstrate the limitations of both Hirsch's list and their own. This reading is from the introduction to the collection of essays.

Instructors may wish to point out that Simonson and Walker begin their introduction by citing two books on American education that appeared in 1987, one of which (E. D. Hirsch's *Cultural Literacy*) is included as a reading in *Constructing Literacies.* Simonson and Walker give a short history of the books that began the controversy over diversity within the curriculum and offer a critique of what E. D. Hirsch and Allan Bloom deem as important for Americans to know. Stating simply that the "Hirsch/Bloom world view is out-dated," Simonson and Walker point to the unassailable fact that American culture always has been and certainly is now a multiculture.

Using Hirsch's Appendix List as their target, Simonson and Walker attack Hirsch for the limitations of the list, pointing out the relatively few terms that have to do with women, food, agriculture, the environment, non-European history, or even plants and animals. Charging that the list is the result of a "particular white, male, academic, eastern U.S., Eurocentric bias," Simonson and Walker then offer the beginnings of a new list in an effort to provide a broader base. Instructors may want to invite students to comment on the critique of Hirsch's list and the decision of Simonson and Walker to offer a list of their own. Initial questions for discussion might follow the lines suggested by the Questions for Reaction and Discussion that ask students to assess whether Simonson and Walker's portrayal of Hirsch is fair.

The Questions for Writing are designed to move students away from the straightforward consideration of the differences in the list and into more complex comparisons about the differences between the monoculturalism advocated by Hirsch and the multiculturalism of Simonson and Walker. Encourage student to examine their own college curriculum and determine how multiculturalism has altered the courses or requirements is an effective way of having students consider these issues in practical terms. If, for example, students must complete a cultural diversity requirement at an institution, what is the form of it? Who determines how the requirement is satisfied and is there any assessment of effectiveness in place? Ask students to investigate how the debates over multiculturalism and Hirsch have been reported in the popular press.

3 . ALAN C. PURVES

"GENERAL EDUCATION AND THE SEARCH FOR A COMMON CULTURE"

from Cultural Literacy and the Idea of General Education, *ed. Ian Westbury and Alan C. Purves. 87th Yearbook of the National Society for the Study of Education (Chicago: National Society for the Study of Education, 1988).*

This essay by Alan Purves, a noted consultant on writing and literacy, was initially designed to introduce a collection of essays from a conference sponsored by the National Society for the Study of Education. The conference was organized to survey a range of opinions on the relationship between cultural literacy and general education; the collection of essays includes a number of opinions that were offered at the conference. While Purves's essay was intended to introduce the essays in the collection; the essay stands alone as a useful survey of the traditional requirements of general education for college students.

In the Questions for Reading, I indicate that students might want to investigate the lines from "The Second Coming" by W. B. Yeats, a poem which at least in part offers a commentary on the destruction of the familiar world by revolution and change. The opening lines of "The Second Coming" form an epigraph to Purves's essay, and instructors might wish to take the opportunity to discuss how epigraphs serve to frame and introduce an essay, and in this case, how the author uses the epigraph to conclude the essay as well. Purves begins his essay with a straightforward definition of general education as the "purposeful attempt to provide a particular group of students with a common core of knowledge, skills, and values." Purves also indicates that the concept of general education is peculiarly American and then suggests that all cultures are, by nature, exclusionary. Observing that cultural literacy may be thought of as language learning, Purves reminds readers of three functions of a language curriculum in a school: the promotion of cultural communication, the promotion of cultural loyalty, and the development of individuality. Purves feels that a Hirschean view of cultural literacy stresses the first two goals and finds this view narrow and restrictive. Purves is particularly concerned with the way in which such a restricted view of cultural literacy fails to account for the importance of science and technology.

Instead of Hirsch's narrow view of cultural literacy, Purves suggests that American culture must be viewed in broader terms and meet several challenges:

- The large number of students of diverse backgrounds enrolled in the American educational system; the functional needs of students and the workplace.
- The technological and scientific nature of society.
- The place of fine arts, physical education, and the practical and technical arts.
- The non-Western and non-masculine aspects of culture.

As a way of helping students consider Purves's point that all cultures are exclusionary, instructors might wish to use the first question in Questions for Writing, which invites students to write about the campus-specific information they had to learn to negotiate when they first arrived on the campus of the school they are attending. Encourage students to talk about expressions, place names, and campus-based slang as a useful way to help students understand the larger issues of Purves's essay.

4. PAULO FREIRE

"THE BANKING CONCEPT OF EDUCATION"

from Pedagogy of the Oppressed, *translated by Myra Bergman Ramos*
(New York: Continuum, 1997 ed.)

Among the most influential twentieth-century books on American education has been Paulo Freire's *Pedagogy of the Oppressed*. Freire's opposition to what he terms a "banking concept of education," the notion that a student is a "piggy bank" into which teachers deposit information, has become a rallying point for many students and teachers who favor education as active and not passive. The Questions for Reading encourage students and teachers to begin consideration of this essay by discussing the responsibilities that teachers and students have. An effective way to prompt a discussion is to simply ask students to list responsibilities for both and comment on what they have listed.

The reading printed here is Chapter Two of *Pedagogy of the Oppressed* and is a discussion of Freire's major concern about the current nature of education. He begins by saying that education suffers from *narration sickness*. Students will need to understand this term fully; "narration sickness" is the scenario in which a teacher is the primary agent or subject and students are passive, listening objects. The drama involves the teacher—not the students. To Freire, the "sonority" of words and not their "transformative" power is at the basis of narrative education. In this system, students memorize mechanically the information that is given to them and education is, therefore, an act of "depositing." One of the most chilling statements that Freire makes is: "The more meekly the receptacles permit themselves to be filled, the better students they are."

To Freire, such a view of education strips students of inquiry, which he regards as a crucial aspect of humanity. "Knowledge," he says, "emerges only through invention and re-invention, through the restless, impatient, continuing, hopeful inquiry human beings pursue in the world, with the world, and with each other." Freire lists a series of attitudes and practices that are the hallmarks of the banking concept of education:

- The teacher and the student have strict roles of behavior.
- The teacher knows everything and students know nothing.
- The teacher thinks and the students are thought about.
- The teacher talks and the students listen.
- The teacher disciplines and the students are disciplined.
- The teacher chooses and students comply.
- The teacher acts and the students have the illusion of action.
- The teachers choose the program and the students adapt.
- The teacher takes on all authority and the students have none.
- The teacher is the subject and the students are the objects.

In the next part of the essay Freire analyzes the results of this educational system and they way in which it is the tool of oppressive governments. Oppression is the hallmark of the banking concept of education, and such a system has no place, in Freire's view, in a democratic society.

To counter the banking concept of education, Freire offers "libertarian education" or "problem-posing education." In this scheme, "acts of cognition" are privileged over "transferrals of information." Students and teachers continually exchange roles and authorities. Education becomes the "practice of freedom" as opposed to the "practice of domination." To Freire, "Problem-posing education, as a humanist and liberating praxis, posits as fundamental that the people subjected to domination must fight for their emancipation. To that end, it enables teachers and students to become Subjects of the educational process by overcoming authoritarianism and an alienating intellectualism; it also enables people to overcome their false perception of reality."

Using this essay as a departure point, instructors may wish to ask students to discuss the views of other writers in this section and consider how they might respond to Freire's "banking concept of education." In my experience, students are eager to discuss their own educational histories in light of Freire's ideas; these experiences can be the preliminary to a fruitful discussion of how institutions internalize various philosophies of education. Instructors should encourage students to avoid simple dichotomous reasoning; for example, in the second Question for Writing, students are asked to consider whether Freire is right to suggest that the relationship between student and teacher is always oppositional and whether there are any instances where the banking concept of education is useful or necessary.

5 . B E N J A M I N   R .   B A R B E R

"AMERICA SKIPS SCHOOL"

Harper's Magazine, *November 1993, pp. 40–48.*

The subtitle of this essay, "Why We Talk So Much about Education and Do So Little" is a useful place for the beginning of a discussion. Instructors might ask students to consider how much time and attention education as an issue receives in the popular press, from politicians, and from citizens. And yet, as Barber points out, we spend much more time talking about education in the United States than we do in taking specific action for improvements and change. Barber takes the provocative stand here that education is finally not truly important to Americans; we pretend to care.

Barber begins by citing a recent report by the Department of Education that more than 90 million adults lack simple literacy skills. Barber observes that such reports always give rise to a flood of political and media commentaries on the current crisis in American education. For Barber who observes that we have an education crisis every dozen years or so, "The education crisis is kind of like violence on television: the worse it gets the more inert we become, and the more of it we require to rekindle our attention." Barber's position is that Americans prefer to look for scapegoats and write about educational problems rather than take action.

Students will be drawn immediately to Barber's "Real-World Cultural Literacy" quiz in the second part of his essay. The results of this quiz, according to Barber, reveals the hypocrisy of our educational system and suggests what we really value in our culture. His conclusion is that "our children's illiteracy is merely our own, which they assume with commendable prowess." Barber spends the second half of his essay discussing "civil literacy" as a fundamental in American society. It, according to him, "encompasses the competence to participate in democratic communities, the ability to think critically and act with deliberation in a pluralistic world, and the emphaty to identify sufficiently with others to live with them despite conflicts of interest and differences in character." Barber then makes a series of recommendations about promoting civil literacy, if, he says, we as a society were really serious about doing so. He suggests raising teachers' salaries, upgrading physical facilities, extending the school year, and involving teachers, parents, and students in solving problems rather than administrators, politicians, and experts. The extent to which we are unwilling to consider these solutions suggests to Barber our lack of interest in solving these problems. We are not, Barber suggests, serious about education in America.

While much of Barber's essay is a sustained attack on recent critiques of American education, he also defends his own view of what the purpose of education should be: the cultivation of civil literacy. Several questions in the Questions for Reaction and Discussion and in the Questions for Writing might be successfully used as the basis for classroom discussion and writing assignments about this view in contrast with the views of other writers in *Constructing Literacies*. Instructors who are interested in incorporating the recent problems of fatal shootings in American schools might encourage students to consider Barber's notion of civil literacy in light of those episodes. Finally, Barber makes some specific recommendations about how public education might be improved. Students might be encouraged to assess their own secondary institutions in light of Barber's recommendation and consider how such recommendations might have changed their own educational environments.

6 . J A M E S   M O F F E T T

"CENSORSHIP AND SPIRITUAL EDUCATION"

from The Right to Literacy, *ed. Andrea A. Lunsford, Helene Moglen, and James Slevin*
(New York: MLA, 1990).

This essay, written by a well-respected authority on writing-across-the-curriculum and the teaching of writing, is a thoughtful discussion drawn from the author's investigation into a 1974 textbook controversy in Kanawha County, West Virginia that resulted in the firebombing of a school. Moffett uses the circumstances surrounding the conflict to consider how threatening a multicultural curriculum is to fundamentalists opposed to the teaching of multiple viewpoints. Moffett provides a careful analysis of the fundamentalist opposition, revealing the fears of many adults that their children will be taught to ignore family and religious values. The controversy reveals the dilemma of a single curriculum for a pluralistic populace; Moffett also provides yet another perspective on the multiculturalism debate.

Moffett begins the essay by explaining the circumstances of his involvement in the West Virginia controversy. Moffett was the author of a K–12 series, *Interaction,* adopted by the school district to fulfill a state mandate on multicultural materials in reading and language arts textbooks. The opposition among fundamentalists was extreme and eventually violent; the protesters charged that the books attacked "family, church, and state—authority in general." Moffett presents the opposition sensitively, careful to be respectful of views that he does not share, and students should be encouraged to notice the tactful way in which he presents opposing viewpoints. After all, the materials that the protesters were attacking were materials that Moffett had spent considerable time and effort organizing and editing.

One of the most interesting parts of Moffett's strategy in this essay is his position that he is committed to spiritual education, what he defines as the perception of "oneness behind the plurality of things, people, and other forms." Educating people to identify with others is a spiritual goal to Moffett, and he suggests that a spiritual education can accomplish moral and religious education without moralizing or indoctrinating. Spiritual education to Moffett is an appropriate middle ground between the excesses of both secularism and fundamentalism. As he says in the conclusion of his essay, "Transmit the culture, yes, but subordinate that to transcending the culture, which after all isn't doing very well right now, like the others. The world is warring right and left because the various cultures strive so intently to perpetuate themselves that they end by imposing themselves on each other.

Instructors might begin discussion of this reading by asking students to explain, in their own words, the dispute that happened in West Virginia. What other incidents involving textbook controversies do students know about? Students might also wish to discuss Moffett's use of "censorship" in this essay. What do they know about the history of censorship involving certain texts, such as *Huckleberry Finn*? Moffett suggests that literacy is dangerous—what do students make of such a statement? Fruitful discussions for students also include asking them to delineate carefully the difference between what Moffett means by spiritual and religious education. Finally, invite the students to read Gina Berriault's "The Stone Boy" and discuss it in a general forum on the text as an effective way to bring the reality of Moffett's experience into your own classroom.

7. SVI SHAPIRO

"A PARENT'S DILEMMA: PUBLIC VS. JEWISH EDUCATION"

Tikkun *(November/December 1996), pp. 59–64.*

This essay was first published in *Tikkun,* a bimonthly magazine of politics, culture, and society from a Jewish perspective. The author of the essay, Svi Shapiro, states his position explicitly at the beginning of the essay; he is a professor who has always supported public education and a Jewish parent who has decided to send his daughter to a Jewish school. The essay is a rationale for his personal decision, but also a thoughtful meditation on how family and religious values are preserved within a culture and on how the public schools are failing in their democratic mission. Shapiro sees the public schools as slipping badly, as a mirror of "the increasing polarization of wealth and opportunity found in the wider society." Schools are, therefore, "far from equalizing opportunities for diverse groups of students . . . [and they] typically reinforce the already existing advantages and disadvantages found in the larger culture."

Shapiro explains how he has wrestled with his commitment to improve and reform public education with his strong wish to send his daughter to a Jewish school. Despite the introduction of multiculturalism into school curricula, Shapiro states that "no multicultural environment can offer the judaically rich, evocative and full experience that would be available to her in a Jewish day school. Only in the environment does Jewishness become a form of life that colors moral expression, joyful celebration, the moments of soulful reflection and sadness, and the days and seasons of the calendar." Concluding his essay with a strong acknowledgement of the importance of the decision he has made as well as the implications, Shapiro comments, "I feel the strong and inescapable claims of the particular in a world that more and more demands a recognition of our universal connectedness and responsibilities."

Students who have read James Moffett's essay on spiritual education may wish to begin discussion of this essay in conjunction with Shapiro's. Instructors might ask how Shapiro's position on the importance of the particular differs from Moffett's position on the importance of identification and connectedness. Another way to begin discussion of this essay is to ask students who attended private schools, especially those with a religious affiliation, to discuss their own experiences in those institutions. As a parent, Shapiro has a strong sense of the "thick" texture of Jewish life that he wants his daughter to experience at her school; students might wish to consider whether their experiences as students fulfilled their parents' expectations. The Questions for Writing encourage comparisons with other essays in this section of *Constructing Literacies,* especially the views of Simonson and Walker and Henry Louis Gates (the next reading in the section). Encouraging students to consider Shapiro's doubts about whether the introduction of multiculturalism within the schools is sufficiently effective will help students compare and contrast his view with those of other writers. Finally, Shapiro mentions two popular recent films, *Clueless* and *Slacker,* both of which include sharp portrayals of life in secondary schools. Instructors interested in incorporating media studies in their courses might consider arranging for a showing of one of both of these films and using them as departure points for discussion and writing assignments.

8. HENRY LOUIS GATES, JR.

"THE DEBATE HAS BEEN MISCAST FROM THE START"

Boston Globe (October 13, 1991).

Henry Louis Gates, Jr. is among the most influential and well-known professors in American education. But his influence extends far beyond the world of higher education; Gates is a "public intellectual," and instructors may wish to discuss with students what that term has come to mean. Although Gates is the author many academic books and essays, the reading here is from a newspaper; instructors may with to point out the context for this fairly short article. Writing for the *Boston Globe,* Gates describes his position on the central issues of multiculturalism in American higher education.

He begins by asking, "What is multiculturalism and why are they saying such terrible things about it?" Gates answers this question by suggesting that the challenges of cultural pluralism have been a part of American culture since the founding of the Republic. Gates briefly describes the history of the debate, citing examples of the history of concerns about the college curriculum and the promotion of national interest. Gates's main point, however, is that "ours is a world that already is fissured by nationality, ethnicity, race, and gender. And the only way to transcend those divisions—to forge, for once, a civic culture that respects both differences and commonalities—is through education that seeks to comprehend the diversity of human culture." The world, Gates says, is multicultural already.

Gates concludes his article with a short survey of African American culture and its own multicultural make-up. Negotiating the one and the many is an age-old challenge, and for Gates, there is no choice but to try.

Instructors might wish to begin a discussion of this essay by asking what Gates means by multiculturalism and if cultural pluralism is a synonymous term. Students might also wish to consider one of the Questions for Reaction and Discussion that asks how Gates uses his own background as an African American to bring a particular perspective to the multicultural debate. Finally, some students may wish to contrast Gates's view with those of other writers in *Constructing Literacies* and consider how a particular writer's background influences his or her perspective on multiculturalism.

9. CLAIRE OBERON GARCIA

"EMOTIONAL BAGGAGE IN A COURSE ON BLACK WRITERS"

The Chronicle of Higher Education, *July 27, 1994, B1.*

Claire Oberon Garcia, a professor at Colorado College, wrote this essay as an "Opinion" piece for *The Chronicle of Higher Education.* An African American who teaches black writers to mostly white students, Garcia recounts her experiences and discusses the "emotional baggage" brought to courses in which mostly white students read the works of minority writers. Although *The Chronicle* is designed for an audience of professors and administrators, students will find this essay engaging to read, especially because of Garcia's effective use of details and examples from her classroom and personal experiences.

Garcia begins her essay with an example from her own teaching experience which illustrates the central point that Garcia wishes to make: that authority is a "double-edged sword" when it comes to a black faculty member teaching black texts to predominantly white students. Garcia finds that her students expect her to have additional insight into these texts, simply because she is black. Her essay is a thoughtful analysis of how faculty members of all races must prepare students for the issues of race that emerge in multicultural classrooms and for the assumptions, values, and beliefs that students bring to these classes.

Instructors may wish to introduce a discussion of this essay by asking students about their response to Garcia's opening anecdote, as suggested in the first Question for Reaction and Discussion. Students might also discuss the ways in which they have learned to read and understand texts written by writers whose race is different from their own and what their classroom experience has been like. In the Questions for Writing, students are invited to assess the techniques Garcia uses in her classroom and are asked to write about their own experiences in working in small groups. Other questions concern the notion of "authority" in the classroom—both the students' and the teachers'. Students might discuss as a group what their claims to authority are based on and then write about what authority students should claim in a classroom.

10. CLARA SUE KIDWELL

"THE VANISHING NATIVE REAPPEARS IN THE COLLEGE CURRICULUM"

Change *(March/April 1991), pp. 19–13*

Offering a history and analysis of the state of Native American studies programs in American colleges and universities, Clara Sue Kidwell, the director of the Native American Studies Program at the University of Oklahoma, suggests that the revival of interest in such programs has come about through cultural diversity requirements in the college curriculum. Kidwell offers a series of interesting perspectives on the importance and place of such requirements in the curriculum. Kidwell, herself a member of the Choctaw/Chippewa tribes, is also concerned with what she terms the "identity crisis" of Native American studies. The crisis is fueled by the variety of expectations of the programs themselves.

For example, Kidwell analyzes the expectations of Indian students who are seeking specific knowledge that will assist them in preparing for professional careers in Indian communities or in establishing their own Native American identities. Non-native students often have a variety of reasons for taking courses in a Native American studies program; Kidwell suspects that some of them think they may find easy courses and little intellectual rigor. At the heart of the identity crisis, however, is the serious issue of whether Indian studies programs should be concerned with professional skills or cultural values. Finally, Kidwell discusses the relatively small number of Native American faculty members on American campuses and the necessity of retaining Native American students (less than 40 percent of Indians who finish secondary school choose to go to college) and training them to be teachers and professors.

Students may be surprised to learn about the expectation that is often imposed on Native American Studies programs to provide professional training for careers in Indian communities. A good place to begin a discussion of this essay might be to ask students what they think the purpose of *any* ethnic studies program should be. Instructors who choose to ask students to write an essay using this article might investigate the ethnic studies programs in place on their own campuses and even invite the director of one or two to meet with the class. The first question in the Questions for Further Exploration invites students to determine whether their campus has a Native American Studies Program and to investigate the purposes and the numbers of faculty members and students involved. Finally, students might wish to do some investigation into the history of Native Americans in higher education by researching the current populations and interests of Indian students.

11. CARLOS E. CORTÉS

"PLURIBUS & UNUM: THE QUEST FOR COMMUNITY AMID DIVERSITY"

Change *(September/October 1991), pp. 9–13.*

This third section of *Constructing Literacies* concludes with this essay by Carlos Cortés, a professor of history. Cortés calls himself an "E Pluribus Unum Multiculturalist," a term that students will want to understand from the beginning of their reading. Instructors may wish to ask students why *E Pluribus Unum* appears on the Great Seal of the United States and why this is an appropriate motto. As the Questions for Reading indicate, students may be helped in their reading of this essay by considering the possibility of having "community amid diversity," as the subtitle of this essay suggests. Certainly some of the other writers in this section have found that a difficult goal to achieve.

Cortés begins the essay by suggesting that colleges and universities face two main questions in addressing what he calls the "Diversity Revolution": "First, how can they help American society makes the best of these inevitable demographic changes? Second, how can they deal more effectively with campus diversity in the quest for better institutional climate and community?" Cortés explains that he finds the answer to both these questions in multiculturalism but because that term has become so loaded, he stipulates his own definition—he is an E Pluribus Unum (EPU) Multiculturalist. In other words, he sees in multiculturalism values the tension between the pluribus values of freedom, individualism, and diversity and the unum values of authority, conformity, and commonality. For higher education, the tensions are even higher because, according to Cortés, the presence of women and persons of nonwhite backgrounds has been greatly expanded. This has led to a "revolution of rising expectations" that assumes that colleges and universities will welcome diversity and will also become more responsive.

Cortés devotes the rest of his article to a discussion of what he considers to be four critical Pluribus Unum areas for the college climate:

- Multicultural curricular reform.
- Ethnic isolation and multicultural integration.
- Language and accent diversity.
- Free speech and campus codes of conduct.

Cortés suggests using these categories as a framework for discussion of the issues and a way for campuses to determine how to handle the most perplexing of these issues, that of free speech and campus codes of conduct.

Instructors might begin a discussion of this section of *Constructing Literacies* by asking students to respond to the title of this essay and determine what Cortés means by EPU Multiculturalism. The Questions for Reaction and Discussion suggest some specific lines of discussion; students will probably gravitate toward Question 7, which asks about free speech and campus codes of conduct. Some of the Questions for Writing encourage students to investigate their own campus code of conduct and to research the current policies on their own campuses. In my experience, this topic almost inevitably leads to a discussion of "political correctness"; as Cortés suggests, many commentators have used this phrase as a way of trivializing efforts by college administrators to overcome prejudice and strengthen multicultural understanding. Instructors may find it effective to ask students for their views on this issue and discuss the examples that Cortés presents. Finally, the Questions for Further Exploration suggest some ways in which interested students might explore other issues raised by Cortés, such as the difficult issue of how campuses handle language gaps between students and their classmates and even between professors and students.

USING THE SUGGESTIONS FOR FURTHER READING, THINKING, AND WRITING TO DESIGN WRITING ASSIGNMENTS FOR SECTION 3

Few issues in higher education have received the media attention that multiculturalism and the curriculum has received in the years since the publication of Allan Bloom's *The Closing of the American Mind* and E. D. Hirsch's *Cultural Literacy*. The influence of both men's ideas has been striking and far-reaching. Allen Bloom's life is the basis of a recent novel, *Ravelstein,* by Nobel-laureate Saul Bellow; Hirsch's program of Core Knowledge has become a staple of many elementary school curricula. Indeed, many current students may have been trained in Core Knowledge curricula in their elementary schools.

The essays in this section of *Constructing Literacies* can serve as a fairly thorough introduction to the topic of the relationship of multiculturalism to general education. Instructors may wish to assign most of the readings as a preliminary to a writing assignment that involves some synthesis and analysis of the views presented. In any case, I suggest beginning with Hirsch as a way to provide students important contextual background for a discussion of multiculturalism. Many of the questions in the Suggestions for Further Reading, Thinking, and Writing suggest ways to combine various readings. For example, the second question raises an issue that several writers touch on-the influence of the media on the goals and purposes of multicultural education. A writing assignment such as this one asks students to probe beyond the readings and consider some contemporary sources. Other assignments, such as Assignment 3, invite students to explore one of the less popular issues in this debate: how campuses handle religious diversity. Using the essays of Moffett and Shapiro as a starting point, interested students can examine how an individual campus handles the promotion of toleration for a variety of religious beliefs. Still other assignments address the popular topic of free speech and codes of conduct; most students find this topic an engaging one, and there are a number of contemporary examples that instructors might bring to class for discussion and an eventual writing assignment.

Sample Writing Assignment

Writing Assignment 3—Investigating (Multi) Cultural Literacy

Read

Selected essays in Section 3, such as Hirsch, Simonson and Walker, Friere, Cortes, and Gates.

Consider

All of the essays in this section argue for a particular position on the question of what students need to learn in school and college, in terms of general knowledge for participation in society. Whether the author is arguing for a "cultural" literacy or a "multicultural" literacy, the authors are all clearly concerned with what we need to know in order to communicate with one another and with society at large.

Plan

Your task is to write an essay in which you argue a position based on one of the following:

   1. E. D. Hirsch believes that an emphasis on skills in our schools has eliminated core knowledge from the curriculum. He

outlines his rationale for adopting a curriculum that includes elements of knowledge (his list of names, dates, events, and terms). Do you agree or disagree with this approach? Why or why not? What writers in this section offer other alternatives? How would you modify Hirsch's position to suit your own notion of what a curriculum should be?

2. Simonson and Walker developed an anthology of essays that responded to Hirsch, and other writers in your text also responded to Hirsch. Their general position is that Hirsch advocates a monocultural approach to education and that the United States is too diverse for such an educational reform movement to work. Do you agree or disagree? Why or why not?

3. Some universities have a "gender and cultural diversity requirement" that stipulates that students must take one or two courses from a list compiled by a college curriculum committee. At one university, the requirement reads: "These courses focus on the formation and diversity of cultural and gender identities and on the way these identities change and interact with one another, both in the United States and throughout the world." Determine whether your own campus has such a requirement and research other such requirements at colleges and universities similar to your own by investigating Web sites and college catalogues. Defend or reject such a requirement, based on your position on how you think multicultural literacy can be achieved.

Research

You will need to use a minimum of **three** outside sources in your essay, one of which should be a printed source that you locate in our library and one of which should be an Internet resource.

Write and Rewrite

Write a draft of you essay. Revise carefully, taking into consideration comments and suggestions that I have made on earlier essays.

Oral Presentations

Each students will give a 6–8 minute presentation in class about their thesis and argument for this assignment. Students are to submit a brief outline of their presentation to me before they give their reports.

continued

Students should not read a paper to us—spend some time thinking about how you want to present material. You may use hand-outs, visual aids, and ask for audience participation. You will be evaluated on the organization of your report, your ability to communicate your ideas clearly and concisely, and the overall effectiveness of your report.

Edit

Make sure that each resource you mention is prepared in correct MLA form and that you include a list of Works Cited at the end of your essay.

Schedule

- November 17—Discuss assignment and essays.
- November 19—Workshop session on essay and discussion.
- December 1—Oral presentations.
- December 3—Oral presentations.
- December 5—Essays due by 5 P.M.

Section 4

CYBERLITERACY

Because of the importance of the increasing shift in our culture from print to screen, I have included this fourth section on what I call "cyberliteracy." The essays and articles in this section of *Constructing Literacies* are taken from a variety of print and electronic sources. The purpose of the section is to provide a range of topics and opinions about the impact of computers and emerging technologies on education, especially higher education. The readings range from theoretical formulations about the changing nature of narrative to the legal and ethical issues involved in using new technologies. Additionally, some of the writers examine how the Internet is changing the notion of a college course or even a campus; others deal with the important issue of access to sophisticated equipment and resources. Many of the writers whose work appear in this section are journalists and very recent college graduates; students may wish to consider the background of these writers and how their backgrounds shape the students' reading of the selection.

1. JANET H. MURRAY

"LORD BURLEIGH'S KISS"

from Hamlet on the Holodeck: The Future of Narrative in Cyberspace
(New York: The Free Press, 1997).

Students don't have to be fans of *Star Trek* to find Janet H. Murray's questions about how electronic communication is altering the nature of narrative, story, and the development of characters fascinating reading. Taking the idea of the "holodeck," the virtual-reality vacation retreat for the characters of *Star Trek: The Next Generation* as her touchstone, Murray explores the changing nature of narrative in her book, *Hamlet on the Holodeck*. Drawing on contemporary interest in science fiction, Murray refers to an array of terms such as "photon weapons" and "tricorders;" instructors may wish to survey their students for their knowledge of science fiction. Murray suggests in her book that science fiction often seems to predict the future; instructors may also wish to encourage some initial discussion about how the prevalence of such things as cellular phones seem to reflect early depictions in science fiction. Students will need to understand Murray's use of "utopian" and "dystopian" literature, and instructors may want to call attention to those terms as necessary vocabulary words for this reading.

Murray begins this reading (the first chapter of her book) with an account of a scene taken from an episode of *Star Trek: Voyager* involving a holodeck excursion taken by Captain Kathryn Janeway. Murray calls the *Star Trek* holodeck "a universal fantasy machine, open to individual programming: a vision of the computer as a kind of storytelling genie in the lamp." "Lucy Davenport," the name that Murray gives to the novel that Captain Janeway enjoys participating in is one of several novels that other characters summon up when they have time for the holodeck. Using the plot line that Janeway develops in her fantasy, Murray discusses and analyzes the impact of the new storytelling forms that provide virtual reality, such as the utopian holonovel outlined here. An alternative form is the descendant of Aldous Huxley's dystopian "feely" of *Brave New World*, with its "dehumanizing and addictive sensation machine." Murray suggests the power and danger of the new "multisensory media": the "populace is overpowered." The utopian and dystopian fictions made possible in new ways by new technologies and offer both hopes and fears of the possibilities of new representational technologies.

The Questions for Reaction and Discussion that follow this reading are designed to help students consider the implications of new technologies on storytelling and narrative and to respond to Murray's provocative observations about the future of digital storytelling. Instructors might wish to encourage students to discuss their experiences with alternative narratives, such as those employed in video or computer games, as well as experiences they may have had in MUDs or other forms of experimental stories, such as hypertext fiction. Writing assignments might well follow the lines suggested in the Questions for Writing; instructors who are interested in incorporating film into their classes may wish to investigate the episodes of *Moonlighting* that are experimental in nature or show the film versions of *Brave New World, Farenheit 451,* or *Lawnmower Man* to launch discussion of the various directions "sensation-based" storytelling might take. Finally, Murray maintains a rich Web site, http://web.mit.edu/jhmurray/www, with links to many resources, including an interview that she has given. Instructors may wish to encourage students to read the hypertext version of "Lord Burleigh's Kiss" on her site and contrast the experience of "reading" it with the experience of reading the printed text of *Constructing Literacies*.

2. LAURA MILLER

WWW.CLAPTRAP.COM.

The New York Times Book Review (March 15, 1998), p. 43.

Laura Miller, an editor for the Internet magazine *Salon,* wrote this opinion piece for the print version of *The New York Times Book Review.* Appearing on the back page of the *Review* as an article in the "Bookend" series, the essay takes its place among articles that are more frequently devoted to extended obituaries of eminent literary figures and meditations on contemporary arts and letters. "www.claptrap.com" is a witty analysis of the so-called "death of the book" essay. Miller surveys a number of hypertextual fictions and concludes that most readers do not wish to be liberated from the author; in fact, readers delight in knowing an author and not in "rearranging" the novel of that author. More suited to contemporary literary theorists than to readers, hyperfiction, in Miller's view, is unlikely to have broad appeal.

Miller's essay makes a good companion to Murray's essay, especially since students will notice that Miller alludes to *Hamlet on the Holodeck* in her article. Although students may not yet have read the essay by Sven Birkerts later in this section, instructors may wish to point it out to students who become interested in the future of fiction and books in electronic culture. Instructors may wish to encourage students who are especially interested in hyperfiction to explore the websites of hypertext fiction (such as Grammatron," http://www.grammatron.com listed in the Questions for Further Exploration.

3. KEVIN HUNT

"THE CULTURAL CURRENCY OF THE BOOK"

CMC Magazine (August 1998). http://www.December.com/cmc/mag/1998/aug/hunt.html

Kevin Hunt's "The Cultural Currency of the Book," was originally published in a now-defunct Internet Magazine, *CMC Magazine,* and appears in *Constructing Literacies* in print for the first time. Hunt's essay is actually a review of David Hudson's *Rewired: A Brief (and Opinionated) Net History,* but more than just a review, Hunt's essay provides a very interesting perspective on the difference between reading books and visiting a Web site. A good place to begin with a discussion of this essay is the title; I like to ask students what they think "cultural currency" means and ask them to determine Hunt's definition from their reading of his review.

Hunt's essay is an interesting assessment of the continual popularity of the book, despite the incursions of the Internet. Despite the relatively wide availability of computers and access to the Internet, people are not, as Hunt says, flocking to URLSs for books online or accessing book webs in large numbers. Hunt points out that economics is, of course, one reason. But an important second reason is that technology has still not evolved to the point where it is very comfortable or especially convenient to read a long text online. But Hunt cites a third reason for the enduring popularity of books—for most of those raised in a print culture, reading a printed book is just a very different experience from reading a website. It's not possible to have a shared experience in using a Web site—each "reader" has a different experience and follows different links. It makes talking about it difficult.

An excellent way to demonstrate some of the points Hunt makes is to assign students some reading in an Internet magazine, such as the ones listed in the Questions for Writing. Asking students to compare their experiences in reading a site as opposed to a printed text is a good way to get students thinking about the differences between print and electronic culture. Students might also discuss books as artifacts—many people collect books—how does this fact contribute to the "social currency" of books? Hunt's essay is a good one to use along with those of Murray and Miller. The third Question for Writing specifically invites students to compare and contrast the views of these three writers. Finally, an effective way to have students examine one of Hunt's contentions, that book webs are already in place, is to assign students the first of the Questions for Further Explorations. Ask them to explore online bookstores and analyze how bookstores are using a variety of features to promote the sale of *printed* books. This a good way to provide first-hand research experience for students interested in this question.

4. SVEN BIRKERTS

"PERSEUS UNBOUND"

from The Gutenberg Elegies: The Fate of Reading in an Electronic Age
(New York: Fawcett Columbine, 1994).

Sven Birkerts is among the most vocal critics of the cultural shift from print to screen in contemporary society. The cover illustration of *The Gutenberg Elegies: The Fate of Reading in an Electronic Age* vividly suggests his position: the image is an inviting armchair in an obviously Victorian-style sitting room. While Birkerts acknowledges the gains of the electronic age but laments a series of losses, especially pointing out estrangement and fragmentation as features of the electronic age. "Perseus Unbound" is the ninth chapter of *The Gutenberg Elegies*. Instructors might want to begin by asking students to recount the mythological story of Perseus, the son of Zeus who explored the limits of the world, slew Medusa, and rescued Andromeda.

The initial topic of this essay is the interactive database, Perseus 1.0, a huge collection of Greek literature, an encyclopedia, a Greek lexicon, and a library of art and archeological images. While Birkerts sees the obvious advantages of such a tool, he worries about the implications of such archives and offers four reservations:

- The allusion of access.
- The loss of narrative structure.
- The sacrifice of depth.
- The ability of anyone to process so much information.

Instructors might want to make sure that students have examined a large database or archive such as Perseus before beginning the discussion of this essay. Many of the archives under construction at the Institute for Advance Technology in the Humanities at the University of Virginia (see http://jefferson.village.virginia.edu/iath) are accessible to students and good examples of the wealth of information that is available to students. Once students understand the nature of these archives, instructors might want to assign one of the Questions for Writing, such as 2, in which students are asked to examine Birkert's claim that there is a distinction between access and wisdom. How does electronic culture make this distinction harder to determine? Another effective assignment is to ask students to pursue the first in the Questions for Further Exploration. The online conference held by the *Atlantic Monthly* for America Online is a good introduction to some of Birkerts's additional concern about the demise of print culture.

5. PAUL ROBERTS

"VIRTUAL GRUB STREET"

Harper's Magazine *(June 1996), pp. 71–77.*

"Virtual Grub Street" by Paul Roberts offers a very different perspective in the print/electronic culture debate. Roberts is a full-time freelance writer who works almost exclusively for CD-ROM companies. Both the title with its allusion to Grub Street, the lowly address of many professional writers in seventeenth and eighteenth century London, and the subtitle of the essay, "Sorrows of a Multimedia Hack," suggests Roberts's attitude toward his profession.

Roberts begins his essay by describing what his current job as a writer for CD-ROMs involves. He's writing about classical composers for a multimedia project on European history, and he explains that although he knows little about such composers, this is an advantage. Because the producers of CD-ROMs expect "small, easily digestible, on-screen chunks" of information, Roberts has come to specialize in the two-hundred word essay. Using his current assignment on classical composers as his departure point, Roberts discusses the effects of this new approach to writing—and alludes to the work of others in this section of *Constructing Literacies*. Roberts explains his job as a multimedia writer as a cog in the machine of CD-ROM production and suggests that his job is not so much as a writer as it is tailoring "specified content into a specified space." The "non-linearity" of the writing Roberts does is perhaps the most important feature; Roberts says that "each blurb must, almost by definition, carry out its minimal literacy function in virtual independence from the rest of the story." Roberts concludes that this new non-linear writing is the wave of the future and that he is taking part in the extinction of the tradition of linear print.

While other writers in this section of *Constructing Literacies* have written about the productions of electronic culture, this essay is different in that Roberts is a writer in the process of *producing* electronic culture. His inside view is a valuable one, and students should be encouraged to examine the difference between an essay that is written for a magazine such as *Harper's* and the examples Roberts gives from his CD-ROMs in the essay. Instructors might also want to point out that Roberts uses his personal experience in this essay to write thoughtfully about some of the larger issues in the move from print to electronic culture. In the Questions for Writing, students are invited to compare Roberts's comments with those of Jay David Bolter, a theorist of electronic culture (as opposed to Roberts who might be considered a practitioner). Finally, students might wish to pursue one of the Questions for Further Exploration and investigate the number and range of CD-ROMs that are currently available, including perhaps, Perseus, the database discussed by Sven Birkerts.

6. KELLY McCOLLUM

"'RAMPING UP' TO SUPPORT 42,000 STUDENT COMPUTERS ON A SINGLE CAMPUS"

The Chronicle of Higher Education *(March 20, 1998),* A27–A29.

This article by Kelly McCollum for *The Chronicle of Higher Education* is a report on how the University of Florida decided to require students to own their own personal computers and what the university hoped to accomplish by this requirement. Selected here as an example of how institutions are coping with the issue of access to computers for students, the article is straightforward and includes some useful summaries of technical information.

Instructors might begin discussion of this article by asking students what they know about the accessibility of computers on their own campuses.

- Are students required to bring their own computers?
- How easy is it to get connected to the Internet in student housing?
- What technical support is available?
- What computer labs are available on campus?
- What are the hours at the computer labs?
- What resources are available to students with limited computer experience? Discussing these questions is a helpful preliminary to considering the larger issues of access and use of resources on any college campus.

The article begins with news of the announcement made by officials at the University of Florida that all 42,000 students would be required to buy own their own personal computers by the fall of 1999. The requirement is seen by the president of the university as "ramping up" the campus. At the time of this announcement, the University of Florida's requirement impacted more students than any other university requirement. McCollum provides helpful background information in the article by explaining how the university intends to manage the transition for technical support and for students and faculty members. McCollum describes in detail the necessary technical adjustments that will need to be made to the campus network, the modem pool, and to university housing. In addition, the university has arranged for Web-based courses on computer topics to help train students, staff, and faculty members. The article concludes with some comments from faculty members about the use of computers in their courses.

The Questions for Reaction and Discussion help students work through the article and process the information that is provided. The Questions for Writing provide opportunities for students to explore more complex issues. For instance, instructors might want to follow the lead offered in Question 1 and note that no student is quoted in the article. In this assignment, students would interview one another as if they were all University of Florida students and determine their reactions to this requirement of the university. Students might then write letters to *The Chronicle* or to the Florida student newspaper about their response and the response of their friends. Other questions encourage students to investigate the requirements at their campuses and others. The first Question for Further Exploration encourages students to do a follow-up investigation on the University of Florida and determine what the aftermath of this decision has been.

7 . T O D D   O P P E N H E I M E R

"THE COMPUTER DELUSION"

Atlantic Monthly *280: July 1997, pp. 45–59.*

As the first Question for Reading indicates, a good way to begin the discussion of this essay is to ask about the specific use of *delusion* in the title. What does the title suggest about the nature of the essay?

- The thesis of this provocative essay is that there is little evidence that the use of computers significantly improve teaching and learning and yet school districts are eagerly embracing new technologies and cutting programs to reallocate resources for them. Oppenheimer criticizes the Clinton administration for its "credulous and costly enthusiasm" and suggests that politicians, school administrators, and many citizens have uncritically accepted computers as crucial to effective teaching and improved learning. Oppenheimer provides a series of examples of school districts that have cut programs to pay for costly computer equipment and provides a series of expert opinions on the uncertainty of how effectively computers can and will be used in the classroom. Oppenheimer sets our five main arguments to computerize the nation's schools:
- Computers improve teaching and learning.
- Computer literacy should be taught as early as possible.
- Learning computer skills is a priority.
- Technology programs should leverage support from the business community.
- Working with computers improves connections with teachers, other students, and other professionals.

Throughout the rest of the article, Oppenheimer assesses the validity of each of these arguments and finds them lacking in evidence and support. As just one example, Oppenheimer provides a good bit of evidence that working on computers and using the Internet may be more isolating to students than actually connecting them to others. Throughout, Oppenheimer quotes a number of well-respected computer industry experts; near his conclusion, he quotes Steven Jobs, the head of Apple Computer, who says, "What's wrong with education cannot be fixed with technology."

Oppenheimer's essay is carefully organized and supported with a wealth of quotations and many observations from his own experience of observing activities in schools. Instructors may want to ask students how persuaded they are by Oppenheimer's persuasive array of support. Students might be encouraged to take one of the five arguments that Oppenheimer dismantles and investigate that argument on their own. The Questions for Writing, for example, suggest some ways in which students might write essays that either provide further support or counter what Oppenheimer has to say. Instructors might also consider inviting a school administrator or an education expert on their own campus to come and speak to the class about computer use in schools. Finally, students might wish to place Oppenheimer's strongly negative view of computers up with others in this section, such as Sven Birkerts or the Gertrude Himmelfarb selection that appears next. For further information on the Clinton Administration's record on computer use and support in the schools, the Questions for Further Exploration offer some ideas.

8. GERTRUDE HIMMELFARB

"A NEO-LUDDITE REFLECTS ON THE INTERNET"

The Chronicle of Higher Education *(November 1, 1996), A56.*

Students may recall the name of Gertrude Himmelfarb from Denise K. Magner's essay, "Professors and Influential Alumni Join Forces to Protect Brooklyn College's Core Curriculum," in Section 2 of *Constructing Literacies.* An alumna of Brooklyn College, Himmelfarb was one of the people who wrote to successfully fight the revision of the Brooklyn College core curriculum. In this essay, Himmelfarb, a well-known scholar of Victorian history and culture, raises concerns about the way in which new technologies are affecting learning and scholarship. Although she alludes to herself as a "neo-Luddite," Himmelfarb makes it clear that she is not opposed to computers or new technologies and cheerfully uses a computer and the Internet for writing, research, and communication.

Students may need some additional assistance with the term, *Luddite,* and with Himmelfarb's qualified use of it. The essay is not what some students might assume—a protest against the use of computers. Himmelfarb presents a brief historical account of the nature of revolutions—the shift from handwritten texts to the printed ones, for example. Himmelfarb's concerns about computers are complex. As an information-retrieval device, Himmelfarb is impressed with how the Internet provides such fast information, but she rightly worries about reliability and validity of information. But it is as a learning device that computers worry Himmelfarb most. Like Birkerts and Oppenheimer, Himmelfarb is concerned about information overload and how students process and manage the huge amont of information, images, and sounds that are instantly available. For social history, Himmelfarb explains that computers are quite valuable, but for studying intellectual history, she is concerned that the kind of laborious reading and study that is necessary for fully understanding difficult concepts is at odds with the instantaneous chunks of information generally available. Like postmodernism, the nonhierarchical Internet does not distinguish between the important and the trivial; all information is presented as of the same value.

Once students have read and understood Himmelfarb's essay, I suggest assigning the letter to the editor from Edward P. Kardas, which appeared in *The Chronicle* a few weeks after the publication of Himmelfarb's essay. Instructors might point out that *The Chronicle* (and most publications) publish many letters to the editor in response to articles and essays. In the example given here, Kardas agrees with part of Himmelfarb's argument but disagrees with another part. In the third Question for Writing, students are encouraged to read Kardas's letter and then compose their own response to Himmelfarb in the form of a letter to the editor. In the Questions for Further Exploration, students are invited to investigate two of the authors Himmelfarb mentions, Michael Kinsley, the editor of the Internet magazine *Slate,* and Elizabeth Eisenstein, author of *The Printing Press as an Agent of Change,* a controversial book about the shift from scribal to print culture.

9. BARBARA KANTROWITZ

"MEN, WOMEN, AND COMPUTERS"

Newsweek *(May 16, 1994), pp. 34–40.*

Barbara Kantrowitz was among the first people to write about and analyze gender differences in the use of computer technology. In 1994 when this essay first appeared, Kantrowitz found that women were disadvantaged in cyberspace; instructors might want to draw students' attention to the first Question for Reading which invites them to consider the differences between men and women as computer users today.

Kantrowitz begins her essay, which was a feature story for the issue of *Newsweek* in which it appeared, with a set of examples of the differences between the men and women respond to and use computers. Clever phrases such as "men and women often seem like two chips that pass in the night" make for entertaining reading. One of the headnotes in the article might serve as a kind of summary of the differences that Kantrowitz finds: "Barbie vs. Nintendo." And much of the article is focused on "girls' technophobia." Kantrowitz summarizes research about boys' interest in computer games and girls' interests elsewhere. She also describes the various efforts of schools to interest girls in computers. Kantrowitz concludes her essay by suggesting that many researchers believe that "we are at a turning point" when it comes to gender differences in cyberspace.

One reason this essay is in *Constructing Literacies* is to demonstrate the importance of historical context, even in a field like cyberliteracy which has a very short history. This essay will strike many students as dated, but for its time (1994—not that long ago) Kantrowitz was reporting on current information. Instructors may want to begin discussion of the essay by inviting comments about how times have changed, what programs have been put in place to assist women in becoming more accustomed to computers, and what students think of as gender differences in cyberspace today. There are a number of current studies of computer games, for example, and students may want to investigate the number of games that have been specifically developed for girls, as a way of studying current gender differences in cyberspace. The Questions for Writing and the Questions for Further Exploration suggest some directions for such investigations.

10. JOHN TIERNEY

"WOMEN EASE INTO MASTERY OF CYBERSPACE"

The New York Times, *December 17, 1998, p. B1.*

Although John Tierney was not specifically writing a response—four years later—to Barbara Kantrowitz, following "Men, Women, and Computers" with this column written for the *New York Times* is an effective way to provide a different perspective on gendered use of computers. Tierney specifically challenges the perception that the Internet is mainly used by men, and instructors may begin an interesting discussion in class by simply inviting students—men and women—to share their experiences of computer and Internet use. The Questions for Reading suggest some directions for this kind of discussion.

Tierney begins his article with the provocative statement that "Women are yet again taking over a medium invented by men." Tierney uses effective statistics (five years ago only 5 percent of Internet users were women and today 50 percent are) and refers to the extremely popular Web site for women: http://www.iVillage.com, a site that students may well wish to visit and explore. Tierney surveys a series of other initiatives begun by women and concludes that the latecomers to the Internet are increasingly a part of a new "army of well-spoken, well-connected women."

A good place to begin discussion of this article is with the two Questions for Reaction and Discussion about the assumptions about women and men that govern this essay. Students may want to discuss the difference in assumptions that Kantrowitz and Tierney use and talk about how those assumptions govern the development of the essays. The Questions for Writing naturally encourage comparisons between Kantrowitz and Tierney by suggesting that students consider what changes have occurred since the publication of the two essays (and what since) and how important computers have become in communication (use of e-mail, chat rooms, and threaded discussions). In the Questions for Further Exploration, some students may want to investigate sites (like iVillage.com) that cater specifically to women and compile a directory for classmates.

11. JOHN N. HICKMAN

"CYBERCHEATS: TERM-PAPER SHOPPING ONLINE"

The New Republic (March 23, 1998), pp. 14–16.

Section 4 of *Constructing Literacies* concludes with an essay that touches one of the many ethical questions that Internet use raises for students. As even a novice can see, the Internet provides vast sources of information and a ready source of already written papers. Long the bane of instructors who assign essays and research papers in courses, mail-order term paper companies have given way to online research paper companies. John N. Hickman, a recent college graduate who is now a working journalist, wrote this essay for *The New Republic* to call attention to the widespread use of these purchased papers among students.

In the Questions for Reading, students are reminded that Hickman assumes that his readers understand plagiarism. Instructors, especially those who are using *Constructing Literacies* in writing courses, may want to take this opportunity to make sure that students understand plagiarism and even to draw their attention to whatever policies the writing program or the college has in place. Many institutions, for instance, have Honor Codes that specifically address plagiarized papers; in many cases the penalties for submitted plagiarized work are very serious. Students who are not aware of such policies should be encouraged to find out about them at this point.

Hickman surveys several Web sites that offer essays and research papers for sale and provides a series of comments about the quality and uses of such papers. Hickman also interviewed several students for this article, and their comments are revealing. Students often resort to plagiarism because:

- They are short on time.
- They don't understand the assignment.
- They aren't engaged in the topics they are to write about.
- They think the paper they are supposed to write is a waste of time.

Hickman also comments on the lawsuit of Boston University against eight research paper companies. Hickman concludes his article by suggesting that the best way for universities and faculty members to reduce the use of plagiarized papers is to have smaller classes and a better student-to-faculty ratio.

In my experience, this article prompts a lively discussion. Hickman's tone is that of the recent graduate, and students are inevitably interested in this topic. In the Questions for Writing, I encourage students to investigate the outcome of Boston University's lawsuit against the online term paper companies (it was dismissed in December 1998). Students may wish to research the suit and consider the implications of the judge's decision to dismiss the case. Students might also wish to study their institutional policies on plagiarism and computer use and evaluate those policies for themselves. Are they fair? Are students adequately trained in the policies? Finally, students may wish to take up the question of freedom of speech and censorship on the Internet and investigate the sites I refer to in the Questions for Further Exploration, such as the Blue Ribbon Campaign, http://www.eff.org/blueribbon.html and the Center for Academic Integrity at Duke University http://www.academicintegrity.org.

USING THE SUGGESTIONS FOR FURTHER READING, THINKING, AND WRITING TO DESIGN WRITING ASSIGNMENTS FOR SECTION 4

The readings in this section of *Constructing Literacies* encourage a variety of ways to think and write about the ways in which computer technology is altering educational practices. Although distance education isn't specifically covered in this section, some students who have had experience with online courses may want to bring this up in class and even write about it in response to the more general question of how technology is changing the nature of a college education (Question 9). Many of the questions in this section ask students to investigate matters of policy and practice about computer use on their own campuses. I have found these practical investigations to be very fruitful for students; they learn about policies on their own campuses and also have an opportunity to consider larger issues at the same time. Several of the questions invite students to consider the issues of access, which is an increasingly important issue in the public schools and continues to be at many colleges and universities. In all of the suggestions for writing offered here, students are encouraged to use the Internet as a part of their research; I also think it is very effective to ask students to conduct surveys of their fellow classmates and friends in order have the experience of some firsthand fieldwork to consider. Finally, many of the suggestions for writing ask students to think hard about the way in which the shift from print to electronic culture is affecting them personally and as students. I always encourage students to talk about the major issues as they seem them—and to comment on both what is being gained and what is being lost.

Sample Writing Assignment

Writing Assignment 4—Cyberliteracy

Read

Read the selections in Section 4 of *Constructing Literacies,* paying special attention to Hunt, Birkerts, Roberts, Himmelfarb, and Hickman.

Plan

Consider the ways in which computer technology has altered or is in the process of altering your college education in one disciplinary area, such as foreign language instruction, first-year composition, physical or biological science, math, social science, or literature. What are your current reading and research habits? How often do you use a computer? The Internet? For what purposes? What is the role of e-mail in your studies? Consider one of the courses your are currently taking and the expectations for the use of the Internet, the campus library, and/or events on the campus itself. What is the role of technology in this course? How is your instructor helping you use technology? How successfully are you meeting the requirements of this course? How successful have your fellow classmates been? What additional training or resources do you need?

Research

Investigate campus policies for Internet use, resources for assistance, technical support available to students (including short courses), and check the online information from other colleges and universities for comparison.

Write and Rewrite

Write an article of 700–900 words for your campus newspaper in which you describe the role of technology in a course you are taking, considering your responses to the questions in the PLAN section above. Although you should describe the course in detail, the purpose of your essay is to use the example of your individual course to discuss and analyze the larger issues of computer use for yourself, other students, and for your campus in general. Use the information you learn from your research and your reading in *Constructing Literacies.*

Oral Presentation

Students will make brief (5 minute) presentations to the class, sketching out the thesis and major supporting details of their essays.

Edit

After your presentation is finished, reread your essay carefully and make final editing and proofreading changes and corrections.

Schedule

- November 17—Discuss assignment and essays.
- November 19—Workshop session on essay and discussion.
- December 1—Oral presentations.
- December 3—Oral presentations.
- December 5—Essays due by 5 P.M.

Section 5

AN EDUCATION OF ONE'S OWN

The final section of *Constructing Literacies* includes a series of perspectives and opinions on a variety of extracurricular aspects of college life and how students can make their college experience their own. Writers in this section deal with a host of issues—students interests and attitudes, extracurricular activities and programs, gender differences and sexual preferences, student activism, career choices, sports programs, and what constitutes a successful learning experience for students. The emphasis throughout is on how a student's variety of additional experiences influences the kind of educational experience he or she may have in college. The range is necessarily broad; instructors may wish to introduce this section by asking students to consider how the activities they participate in reflect their interests and what steps they take to try new ones. One effective way to encourage students to investigate the range of activities offered by any college campus is to ask students to attend or participate in a campus event that would not normally appeal to them and write an e-mail message to the members of their class reporting on it. I have had some very successful experiences with this assignment, despite initial grumbling. After one student who told me that he would never consider studying abroad attended a session designed to acquaint students with the program, he changed his mind and spent a semester of his junior year in Spain. Other students have discovered the campus theatre, the campus TV station, and even the campus basketball program. One student told me in an e-mail message at the end of his writing course that my assignment asking students to attend an event they wouldn't normally attend and write about it had been an "inspired" idea.

Inspired or not, asking students to familiarize themselves with campus programs is an effective introduction to this last section which encourages students to think about the ways in which they can structure their own educational experiences. The section begins with the summary of a survey of first-year students' attitudes, abilities, and activities conducted each year by UCLA. The section concludes with a thoughtful chapter from Jane Tompkins's book about how she, as a veteran college professor, has come to view the traditional college classroom.

1 . THE CHRONICLE OF HIGHER EDUCATION

"THIS YEAR'S FRESHMEN: A STATISTICAL PROFILE"

The Chronicle of Higher Education, *January 29, 1999, pp. A37–39.*

Every year, this survey of freshman attitudes, interests, opinions, goals, and activities is conducted and published by the Higher Education Research Institute at the University of California—Los Angeles. I have used this survey in every writing course I have taught since I first discovered its existence in the mid 1980s and have always found it appealing and even engrossing to college students. The purpose of the survey is to provide information to colleges and universities, and even a casual reader of the survey can find out a great deal about first-year students in general. The surveys also reflect shifting patterns of behavior; for example, the survey printed here was from 1999. For the first time, students were asked about their use of e-mail. Instructors who wish to examine the current survey results should check *The Chronicle of Higher Education,* which publishes the survey in mid-January of every year and generally provides a commentary on it. Copies of the full report are also available directly through UCLA.

Instructors will want to introduce the survey by making sure that everyone in the class understands how to read the graphs and charts. I have sometimes been surprised at the limited skills even sophisticated students possess in understanding charts. In any case, most instructors will probably find that spending at least a little time in class looking through the survey with students and talking about different points of information along the way will help students understand and process the information presented here.

Using the Questions for Reaction and Discussion is a good way to facilitate discussion after the students have had an opportunity to study the survey on their own. Asking students to comment on the most surprising piece of information, for instance, can lead students to other observations that struck them as they read the survey. I always ask students to examine the section devoted to what students expect to major in and ask why this is important information for a college or university to know. That question can lead naturally to a quick survey of the class about the majors represented there.

The Questions for Writing provide a series of ways in which students can use parts of the survey to develop topics for essays. Question 1, for example, asks students to compare the education and background information on students' fathers and mothers and suggests a comparison between students' own experiences and those who were surveyed. Question 2 asks students to investigate the reasons students select a particular school. Question 4 asks students to construct a profile of a typical college freshman and consider what the implications are for the student and for colleges in general. The Questions for Further Exploration suggest ways in which students might conduct further research about past surveys.

2 . BEN GOSE

"'U. OF CHICAGO SOCIAL LIFE' MAY NO LONGER BE AN OXYMORON"

The Chronicle of Higher Education, *November 15, 1996, pp. A49–50.*

Students may be amused by the article from *The Chronicle of Higher Education* that reports on the serious efforts of the University of Chicago to improve and expand the social life for students there. As Ben Gose explains, many administrators are concerned that students should be more integrated into the community at Chicago, and the article is a report of their initiatives. As Gose explains, Chicago has expanded its student union and added a number of coffee shops, all in an effort to improve social life on the campus and to attract more undergraduates to the distinguished research university. Gose quotes a number of students in the article, and the students's comments are generally negative about the efforts of the administration to change and expand social opportunities. Much of the article is devoted to the efforts of Chicago to expand its undergraduate enrollment and marketing itself differently. The article concludes with the comments of one student who is opposed to the expansion and the changes.

Instructors might begin discussion of this intriguing report by asking students what particular problems the University of Chicago faces in cultivating more social experiences for students. Are these problems similar or different to problems on your own campus? Several of the people quoted in the Gose article comment on the lack of a center for the Chicago campus. Is that true of your own? Why or why not? These questions can lead to the most important issue raised in this article: What is the relationship between a good social experience and a good educational experience? The Questions for Writing invite students to explore the extent to which their own campus facilitates a social life for students and encourages them to consider the larger implications of a successful social life as integral to an educational experience. The Questions for Further Exploration suggest some ways to research the social facilities at other campuses.

3. AMERICAN ASSOCIATION
OF UNIVERSITY WOMEN

"THE ABSENCE OF GIRLS
IN THE CURRENT DEBATE ON EDUCATION"
AND "ACHIEVEMENT AND PARTICIPATION:
WHAT DO THE DATA SHOW?"

from How Schools Shortchange Girls: The AAUW Report: A Study of Major Findings on Girls
and Education *(Washington, D.C.: American Association of University Women Educational
Foundation and National Education Association, 1992).*

4. AMERICAN ASSOCIATION
OF UNIVERSITY WOMEN

"COURSE-TAKING PATTERNS"

from Gender Gaps: Where Schools Still Fail Our Children
*(Washington, D.C.: American Association of University Women Educational Foundation
and National Education Association, 1998).*

These two readings, both from reports commissioned by the American Association of University Women, are collected here to form a unit with the next
essay by Judith Kleinfeld, on the impact of gender on a student's preparedness
for college and for a student's choice of a college major and a career. The
AAUW reports present their findings about the gaps in opportunity for women
and girls; Judith Kleinfeld offers a different reading of much of the research
that is given in these two reports. Instructors may wish to assign the two
AAUW reports, conduct discussions and some preliminary writing assignments, and then immediately introduce the Kleinfeld essay as a counter or follow-up for discussion and writing.

The AAUW has a long history of commissioning an publishing reports
that promote education and equity for women and girls, beginning in 1885
with their report on the prevailing opinion that higher education was damag-
ing to the health of girls. The excerpts reprinted here, from the 1992 report,
*How School Shortchange Girls: The AAUW Report: A Study of Major Find-
ings on Girls and Education,* and the 1998 report, *Gender Gaps: Where
Schools Still Fail Our Children.* The first report was commissioned in response
to the lack of specific information on girls that was a part of a series of national educational reports that were published in the 1980s and the concern that
the experience of girls in the educational process was markedly different from

that of boys. *How Schools Shortchange Girls* concluded with a set of recommendations to the schools that insured the both boys and girls are prepared for the future. The follow-up report, *Gender Gaps,* provided a discussion of the progress that had been made since the 1992 report and to determine what new issues in gender equity had arisen.

The selection printed in *Constructing Literacies* from *How Schools Shortchange Girls* begins with a survey of how girls were omitted from the general discussions about the state of public education in the 1980s. A variety of statistics are presented that demonstrate the number, for example, of male versus female school superintendents and principals. The next section provides a discussion of what studies have shown about achievement and participation in verbal skills, writing, and mathematics and science. This selection concludes with a section on "Implications," which shows some interesting patterns which have developed. The gender gap, for instance, is closing in math achievement but not in science.

The selection from *Gender Gaps* printed here begins with a discussion of "course-taking patterns," which reviews the uneven participation of girls and boys across the entire curriculum. Taking on the goals that were enumerated in the first report, the authors discuss the emphasis on math and science for girls, changes in graduation requirements (including computer-related studies, English, social studies, foreign languages, fine arts, and health and physical education). In addition, the report studies the nature of remedial and special education and suggests that girls are likelier than boys to have their abilities overlooked, but that nonwhite and nonaffluent students (boys and girls) are mostly likely to be placed in remedial classes. The report also studies advanced placement and gifted programs. This reading concludes with a new set of recommendations for improving participation rates for girls in math and science.

The Questions for Reaction and Discussion given at the end of the two readings are designed to be used in a discussion of both the 1992 and 1998 reports. Students should be encouraged to ask about any terms they don't understand; I always make a point of explaining that Title IX of the Education Amendment of 1972 explicitly prohibits discrimination on the basis of sex in any educational program receiving federal funding. But it is important for students to understand that federal enforcement of this Act is complaint-driven, and there remain many inequities even under this law. Students should also be encouraged to study the charts carefully and to make comparisons between the reports. Question 8, for instance, asks students to consider how the course-taking patterns of 1998 differ from those of 1992. Instructors will want to take care in guiding discussions of these reports not to lose the male members of the class; in the Questions for Writing that are outlined here, I have stressed repeatedly the relationship between the experience of girls and boys in this report. At the same time, Question 2 asks students to consider specifically how girls are treated in classrooms. But this question and Question 4 can certainly be addressed by male students. Finally, a Question for Writing that has always resulted in interesting essays for me has been Question 6, which asks students to consider the advantages and disadvantages of single-sex schools. When I use this question, I like to assign a few students to work together to research the advantages and disadvantages. The Questions for Further Exploration direct students to other resources and additional studies about gender equity in schools.

5. JUDITH KLEINFELD

"STUDENT PERFORMANCE: MALES VERSUS FEMALES"

The Public Interest *134 (1999): 3–20.*

In order to demonstrate how controversial the AAUW reports have been to students, I have included here the response of a highly articulate critic of the AAUW, Judith Kleinfeld, a professor of psychology at the University of Alaska, Fairbanks. As I explain in the headnote to this reading, Kleinfeld was encouraged by the Women's Freedom Network to write a position paper, which resulted in her "The Myth that Schools Shortchange Girls: Social Science in the Service of Deception." A later version of this essay (and the one that is printed here) appeared in *The Public Interest,* a journal of conservative interests.

Kleinfeld's essay begins with the challenging statement that "Women's advocacy groups have waged an intense media campaign to promote the idea that 'school shortchange girls.' Their goal has been to convince the public that women are 'victims' of an unfair educational system and that they deserve special treatment, extra funding, and heightened policy attention." From there, Kleinfeld specifically attacks the reports of the AAUW, *How Schools Shortchange Girls* and *Gender Gaps.* Commenting that the AAUW has rightly done women and the nation a service by pointing out the gender gap in math and science, Kleinfeld asserts that many of the findings of the AAUW are misleading or false and that even the comments on math and science need to be put in perspective.

Kleinfeld spends the rest of her essay providing counter examples, additional studies not cited by the AAUW, and different readings of some of the studies used by the AAUW. For example, Kleinfeld points to recent studies undertaken by the Educational Test Service and says that indeed male students do perform better in math and science standardized test but the difference is shrinking quickly and dramatically. Kleinfeld provides a different account of the central position of the AAUW that schools shortchange boys. In her view, "Just as the greater number of males at the top in science and mathematics does not necessarily mean that the schools are shortchanging girls, so too the greater number of males at the bottom in special-education classes does not necessarily mean that the schools are shortchanging boys. The fact is that males are more variable than females on many neurological dimensions."

Kleinfeld also points to an important gender gap that the AAUW does not mention—in college attendance and graduation. African American males are in the most at-risk group of students for dropping out of college. Kleinfeld continues throughout her essay to provide careful documentation of her points and counter points and concludes that while the AAUW has done important work in calling attention to the gender gap in math and science, other groups, such as African American males, may lose out on attention and resources. Kleinfeld's final statement, that teachers "are overlooking the problems of boys," is a powerful last statement of her position.

Instructors may wish to use the first Questions for Reaction and Discussion following the reading to begin discussion of Kleinfeld's essay. Ask students if they find Kleinfeld's introduction effective and why, and ask them if they agree or disagree. In addition, instructors may want to discuss the issues of authority and credibility—how does Kleinfeld establish hers? In what ways do the writers of the AAUW report establish theirs? The Questions for Writing suggest several directions that students might take in working through Kleinfeld's response to the AAUW report. Students might compare the evidence used by Kleinfeld and the AAUW on a particular point (such as evidence of gender discrimination in grades, class rank, and academic honors and prizes). Or students might take Kleinfeld's major point that African American males are the most disadvantaged group in American schools and research this question using Kleinfeld's sources and others that they find. Students might also conduct their own field studies, along the lines of Question 5, and share their findings with their classmates. The Questions for Further Exploration give a series of possibilities for researching the question of gender equity—for both males and females—using both print and electronic resources.

6.   ROBERT A. RHOADS

"GAY LIBERATION AND THE PASSAGE OF THE SEXUAL ORIENTATION CLAUSE AT PENN STATE"

from Freedom's Web: Student Activism in an Age of Cultural Diversity
(Baltimore: The Johns Hopkins University Press, 1998).

For many students, the act of defining an education of one's own also means learning how to stand up for one's beliefs and work to make necessary changes. Student activism is an important way in which students can learn how to effect policy changes. This essay, taken from a chapter of Rhoads's excellent book on a variety of case studies about student activism, narrated the account of how a group of gay students worked to pass a sexual orientation clause to the statement of nondiscrimination at the Pennsylvania State University. Instructors might begin the discussion of this essay by asking students what they know about nondiscrimination statements and sexual orientation clauses. Instructors might also ask about what role students believe they should take at their institutions when it comes to decision-making and policies.

Rhoads begins this essay with an anecdote about a group of students traveling from Penn State to Washington, D. C. to join a 1993 march for lesbian, gay, and bisexual equal rights and liberation. Rhoads contrasts the good spirits and camaraderie of the students on the trip to Washington with the hostile scene that had occurred in front of the student center at Penn State as the group was leaving for the capital. The anecdote serves to introduce the readers to the battle for gay liberation that had been fought at Penn State over the last several years. Immediately following this anecdote, Rhoads recounts the difficult history of Penn State with its lesbian, gay, and bisexual students, beginning with an event in 1972—the removal of a gay student, Joseph Acanfora, from his student teaching assignment. The account of his fight to obtain teacher certification and the development of the Lesbian, Gay, and Bisexual Student Alliance, a national organization with chapters on hundreds of campuses, forms the background for the rest of Rhoads's essay, which concerns the actions of the LGBSA, some faculty members, and some administrators to the passage of a sexual orientation clause. Rhoads details the homophilia at Penn State and the many struggles by various groups on the campus to oppose and support the clause. A faculty member provided an important comparison (between the persecution of Jews and gay men and lesbians) and students threatened a takeover of the President's office. The students were successful in seeing the addition of the clause to the nondiscrimination statement, and Rhoads explains that the passage of this statement was a major step toward creating a more positive climate on the Penn State campus for the lesbian, gay, and bisexual community.

Instructors might lead a discussion of this reading by asking some of the Questions for Reaction and Discussion, especially Question 4, which asks students to delineate carefully the objections to the original wording of the nondiscrimination statement and the comments of Professor Ginzberg. Student may also want to discuss the role of students in changing policies at their own institutions. What are the mechanisms for making change on your campus? The Questions for Writing encourage students to find out about organizations on their own campus that provide services and resources for gay and lesbian students. In addition, students may wish to investigate the presence or absence of nondiscrimination policies on their own campuses and discuss the wording and the implications in some detail. The Questions for Further Exploration suggest some Internet resources for lesbian and gay students.

7. D. STANLEY EITZEN

"BIG-TIME COLLEGE SPORTS"

Vital Speeches of the Day *(December 1, 1997), pp. 122–6.*

Few aspects of college life receive as much attention as intercollegiate athletic programs. As I say in the headnote, these programs unite the student body, divide the faculty, and provide immediate institutional identification for entire regions. With over fifteen percent of college students participating in varsity sports and a much higher percentage attending games of all kinds, college sports is indeed "big-time." There are, as most faculty members know, many demands and pressures on student athletes; it's a topic about which virtually everyone in a college community has an opinion. Instructors might begin a preliminary discussion of this reading by asking students to comment on what they know about intercollegiate athletics on their own campus and how important it is to campus life.

This reading is actually a speech, given by D. Stanley Eitzen, a retired sociology professor. Instructors may want to talk with students about some of the differences between a speech and an essay (this speech was not revised and represents the comments that Eitzen actually made to the Kansas Sociological Society on October 9, 1997). Eitzen's thesis is that "big-time" university sports programs compromises the value of higher education; he discusses in detail the problems of sports as big business, the domination of sports for men, the professionalism in the guise of amateurism, and the pressures on college athletes that seem to foster deviant behavior.

Eitzen begins his speech by making it clear that he loves sports and is speaking as a concerned fan. Eitzen's target here is what he calls "big-time" sports, especially men's football in the 106 Division 1-A schools and men's basketball in the 305 Division 1 schools. One of the advantages of using this speech in a class is that Eitzen provides so many examples and detailed information about college sports; students may be surprised by some of the statistical information he presents. For example, students who have read Judith Kleinfeld's essay in response to the AAUW reports (earlier in Section 5 of *Constructing Literacies*) and noted her concerns about the inattention to African American males in schools, may wish to note with special care the statistics that Eitzen presents here about African American males and their participation in college athletics. Eitzen also discusses the dominance of males in general in college sports and points to the lack of gender equity in college sports, despite the passage of Title IX of the 1972 Education Act. Throughout the speech, Eitzen provides detailed evidence in support of his position that big-time sports do not have a place at academic institutions.

Students are undoubtedly going to have strongly positive or negative responses to this speech. The Questions for Reaction and Discussion suggest some ways of channeling those responses into productive debate and discussion for the class as a whole. Encourage students to think about Eitzen's evidence carefully, regardless of which position they take about his speech. The Questions for Writing suggest some ways in which students can make this topic their own—by interviewing student athletes and by suggesting directions for further research. Students may also wish to learn about athletics on their own campuses—the degree of participation, support services for athletes, graduation rates, and other information that is readily available. Finally, the Questions for Further Exploration suggest that students may wish to access the NCAA Web site www.ncaa.org, a site that provides a wealth of information about college athletics.

8. KATHLEEN GREEN

"TRADITIONAL DEGREES, NONTRADITIONAL JOBS: A DEGREE IS NOT A LIFE SENTENCE"

Occupational Outlook Quarterly *41 (Spring 1997): 12–19.*

Students often become very concerned in their college careers about choosing a major or a field of student that will lead directly to the career they have planned for themselves. Kathleen Green, a lawyer by training, suggests that many people end up with very different careers than the one they trained for and are still leading successful and happy lives. In this essay, Green discusses the experiences of a nurse, an engineer, and a lawyer who transferred their skills and training into other jobs. The purpose of the essay is to convince readers that a "degree is not a life sentence" and indeed, that many people, especially in the contemporary world will change jobs and careers, regardless of their training. Throughout the essay, Green provides examples and quotations from the people she interviewed. At the end of the article, Green provides some suggestions for resources that can help students and job-seekers learn more about careers they are considering.

Instructors might link the topic of this article to the choices of majors that students are considering within the class. The Questions for Reaction and Discussion suggest some directions for this discussion, especially in polling the members of the class to determine what their current thinking is. Students might also discuss the ways in which the people in Green's essay are alike and different; what influences some people to change careers or jobs?

The Questions for Writing are designed to encourage students to investigate resources on their own campuses for career planning. Instructors may wish to invite a staff member from the career or placement center on the campus to speak to the class about the resources available and to provide updated information about career patterns. Students might interview the speaker and use the information as the basis for a response to Question 1. Other questions, including the Questions for Further Exploration, direct students to a variety of additional information resources for helping them consider what majors and fields of study they might undertake.

9 . JANE TOMPKINS

"THE CLOISTER AND THE HEART"

from A Life in School: What the Teacher Learned *(New York: Addison-Wesley, 1996).*

The final reading in this section of *Constructing Literacies* is from Jane Tompkins's *A Life in School: What the Teacher Learned,* partly a memoir of her life as a student and a teacher in higher education and partly a critique of contemporary higher education. As I suggest in the headnote, Tompkins believes that higher education is too much of a passive experience for students, with the teacher as the central authority. Using the "cloister" as a central metaphor in this section, Tompkins meditates on the implications for students, educators, and parents.

Instructors might begin discussion of this reading by asking students what they understand by *cloister* and whether they think their own campus is one. Tompkins begins her essay by examining the schools of her own experience—Bryn Mawr College, Temple University, and Duke University—and briefly considers them as examples. But Tompkins moves on to examine the responses of her own undergraduate students and the ways in which they choose the schools they attend. But Tompkins's major purpose in this essay is to talk about the nature of the college classroom, and she presents a series of examples and vignettes from her own experience to demonstrate her point that "classroom learning can constrict a person's horizons even as it broadens them." Tompkins worries that traditional classrooms promote rote thinking and rote learning; her concern is that the educational system fails to help students find out who they are and where they might use their talents. Tompkins's conclusion is that higher education should be less about training for a career and more about training for life.

The Questions for Reaction and Discussion encourage students to consider their own experiences in classroom learning and to comment on their own notions of the "cloister" as an image for college. Asking students to consider an alternative title for this essay, "The Cloister and the World" instead of "The

Cloister and the Heart" is an effective way to have them delineate some of Tompkins's major assumptions underlying this reading. The Questions for Writing guide students into other ways of thinking about Tompkins's essay. In the first, students are asked to write an essay on a revision of the subtitle of Tompkins's book: what the student learned in school. Instructors who earlier assigned Paulo Friere's "The Banking Concept of Education" in Section 3 of *Constructing Literacies* may wish to ask students to consider how ideas such as Friere's may have influenced Tompkins. Students might also write a detailed account of the climate of a classroom in a course they are currently taking and respond in this way to Tompkins suggestion that students "learn too well the lessons of the classroom." The Questions for Further Exploration encourage additional resources for considering Tompkins ideas.

USING THE SUGGESTIONS FOR FURTHER READING, THINKING, AND WRITING TO DESIGN WRITING ASSIGNMENTS FOR SECTION 5

Instructors who are looking for an effective assignment to help students synthesize many of the perspectives offered in this section might want to consider using Suggestion 1 as a starting point. Since many of the writers presented in this section offer strongly-felt opinions about how a variety of aspects of college affect students, students might want to consider how relevant the views are to them—as students at the beginning of the twenty-first century. Other suggestions offered here provide guidelines for using readings together—such as those of Rhoads, Eitzen, and Gose—who discuss the affects of particular aspects of student life on the educational process itself. What other aspects of student life not covered here (the Greek system, religious activities, or volunteerism) might be investigated? The annual survey of freshmen, offered at the beginning of this section, is a useful source of information for all of the suggestions listed here. Suggestions 6 and 8 provide some ideas for using different sections of the survey as departure points. Finally, instructors may want to consider using Suggestion 10 as a summary writing activity. Taking the title of this section "An Education of One's Own," students are invited to write an assessment of their own educations so far.

SAMPLE WRITING ASSIGNMENT

Writing Assignment 5—A Group Project

Topic

Accommodation of diverse religious perspectives on campus.

Reading/Research Required

Divide the class into writing groups. Each group will collect data on student religious backgrounds from "This Year's Freshmen"; at least one current periodical article (in electronic or print form) about religious activities, practices, and/or facilities on college and university campuses; and at least one primary research source (for example, a survey of students on campus or an interview with a campus minister). Groups may also find it necessary to do some background research on the beliefs and practices of major religions.

Length of Completed Paper

4–5 pages.

Format/Documentation Style

A formally structured paper (introduction containing thesis statement, body, conclusion, and a works cited page). Include survey results, interview questions, observation reports, etc. in an Appendix.

Special Requirements for Group Project

Members of each writing group will work together to produce one paper, with all members of the group receiving the same grade. Each group is responsible for its own division of labor, but every member of the group must make a significant contribution to the project. Each paper must be submitted with a cover letter explaining the nature of the project and the role played by each group member.

Deadlines

Initial group meetings: Week 11
Proposal (including outline, labor-division plan, and working source list) due for instructor approval: Week 12
Draft due for meeting with instructor: Week 13
Completed project due: Week 15

More Information about the Topic

According to an article by Beth McMurtrie in *The Chronicle of Higher Education*, soon-to-be-published results of a study of religion on college campuses suggest changing student perspectives on religion: "Religion is thriving on college campuses, but in forms that previous generations of students may not recognize, stressing spiritual exploration over formal worship." In addition to these changing perspectives on religion, McMurtrie writes in another article, colleges and universities are struggling to meet the needs (in terms of religious activities and facilities for them) of an increasing diversity of student religious backgrounds, beliefs, and practices. Your mission is to draft a paper in which you make recommendations for the development or improvement of religious programs and facilities on your campus in a effort to better serve the needs of a religiously diverse student body. (The first article, "Religion, in Many Forms, Abounds on College Campuses, Study Finds" can be found in the November 23, 1999 issue of *The Chronicle*; the second, "Pluralism and Prayer Under One Roof," can be founded in the December 3, 1999 issue.)

Step-by-Step Instructions

1. Review the religious-affiliation data in "This Year's Freshman" and think about the questions raised in Item 6 of "Suggestions for Further Reading, Thinking, and Writing" at the end of Section 5 in Constructing Literacies.
2. Read the McMurtrie articles and do some preliminary research to develop ideas about what sources are available and how to approach the topic.
3. Meet with your group to discuss the project, make plans, and begin your investigation.
4. Draft an outline, divide up the work for the project, and compile a working list of sources.
5. Submit your proposal to the instructor for approval.
6. Work together to produce a rough draft.
7. Meet as a group with the instructor to discuss the draft.
8. Revise the paper and write the cover letter.
9. Turn in the completed project for evaluation.

III

SELECTED PRINT AND ELECTRONIC RESOURCES FOR INSTRUCTORS AND WRITING PROGRAM ADMINISTRATORS

PRINT

Aronowitz, Stanley. *Education Still Under Siege.* 2nd ed. Toronto: OISE Press, 1993.
———. *Education Under Siege.* London: Routledge & Keegan Paul, 1986.
Ballenger, Bruce. *Beyond Note Cards: Rethinking the Freshman Research Paper.* Westport, CT: Boynton/Cook, 1999.
Barton, David. *Literacy: An Introduction to the Ecology of Language.* Cambridge, MA: Blackwell, 1994.
Belanoff, Pat and Marcia Dickson, eds. *Portfolios: Process and Product.* Westport, CT: Boynton/Cook, 1991.
Bishop, Wendy, ed. *The Subject is Writing.* Westport, CT: Boynton/Cook, 1999.
Bogel, Fredric V. and Katherine K. Gottschalk, ed. *Teaching Prose: A Guide for Writing Instructors.* New York: W.W. Norton, 1984.
Brandt, Deborah. *Literacy as Involvement: The Acts of Writers, Readers, and Texts.* Carbondale, IL: Southern Illinois University Press, 1990.
Brinkley, Alan, et al. *Chicago Handbook for Teachers: A Practical Guide to the College Classroom.* Chicago: University of Chicago Press, 1999.
Crowley, Sharon. *Composition in the University: Historical and Polemical Essays.* Pittsburgh: University of Pittsburgh Press, 1999.
Daniels, Harvey A. *Not Only English: Affirming America's Multilingual Heritage.* Urbana, IL: National Council of Teachers of English, 1989.
Deibert, Ronald J. *Parchment, Printing, and Hypermedia: Communication in World Order Transformation.* New York: Columbia University Press, 1997.
Dethier, Brock. *The Composition Instructor's Survival Guide.* Westport, CT: Boynton/Cook, 1999.

Dixon, Kathleen, ed. [With William Archibald and Jane Varley] *Outbursts in Academe: Multiculturalism and Other Sources of Conflict.* Westport, CT: Boynton/Cook, 1998.

Downing, David B., ed. *Changing Classroom Practices: Resources for Literacy and Cultural Resources.* Refiguring English Studies series. Urbana, IL: NCTE, 1994.

Foehr, Regina Paxton and Susan A. Schiller, eds. *The Spiritual Side of Writing: Releasing the Learner's Whole Potential.* Westport, CT: Boynton/Cook, 1997.

Fulwiler, Toby, ed. *The Journal Book.* Westport, CT: Boynton/Cook, 1987.

Geisler, Cheryl. "Exploring Academic Literacy: An Experiment in Composing." *College Composition and Communication* 43.1 (1992): 39–54.

Gilyard, Keith, ed. *Race, Rhetoric, and Composition.* Westport, CT: Boynton/Cook, 1999.

Graff, Harvey. *The Labyrinths of Literacy: Reflections on Literacy Past and Present.* Pittsburgh, PA: University of Pittsburgh Press, 1995.

Graves, Richard L, ed. *Writing, Teaching, Learning: A Sourcebook.* Westport, CT: Boynton/Cook, 1999.

Hamilton, Sharon Jean. *My Name's Not Susie: A Life Transformed by Literacy.* Westport, CT: Boynton/Cook, 1995.

Handa, Carolyn, ed., *Computers and Community: Teaching Composition in the Twenty-First Century.* Portsmouth, NH: Boynton/Cook, 1990.

Hawisher, Gail and Cynthia Selfe. *Passions, Pedagogies and 21st Century Technologies.* Provo, UT: Utah State University Press, 1999.

Himley, Margaret. [With Kelly Le Fave, Allen Larson, Susan Yadlon, and The Political Moments Study Group] *Political Moments in the Classroom.* Westport, CT: Boynton/Cook, 1997.

Keller-Cohen, Deborah. *Interdisciplinary Conversations.* Cresshill, NJ: Hampton Press, 1994.

Kutz, Eleanor. *Language and Literacy: Studying Discourse in Communities and Classrooms.* Westport, CT: Boynton/Cook, 1997.

Lankshear, Colin. *Literacy, Schooling, and Revolution.* NY: Falmer, 1989.

Leki, Ilona. *Understanding ESL Writers: A Guide for Teachers.* Westport, CT: Boynton/Cook, 1992.

Lindemann, Erka. *A Rhetoric for Writing Teachers.* 2nd Ed. New York: Oxford University Press, 1987.

Macedo, Donaldo. "Literacy for Stupidification: The Pedagogy of Big Lies." *Harvard Educational Review* 63.2 (1993): 183–206.

Malinowitz, Harriet. *Textual Orientations: Lesbian and Gay Students and the Making of Discourse Communities.* Westport, CT: Boynton/Cook, 1995.

McCracken, Nancy Mellin and Bruce C. Appleby, eds. *Gender Issues in the Teaching of English.* Westport, CT: Boynton/Cook, 1992.

McLaren, Peter. "Critical Literacy and Post Colonial Praxis: A Freirian Perspective." *College Literature* 19.3/20.1 (1992/1993): 7–27.

Miller, Richard E. "'Let's Do the Numbers': Comp Droids and the Prophets of Doom," *Profession 99.* New York: MLA, 1999.

Moss, Andrew and Carol Holder. *Improving Student Writing: A Guidebook for Faculty in All Disciplines.* Pomona, CA: California State Polytechnic University, 1988.

Murray, Donald. *Expecting the Unexpected: Teaching Myself—and Others—to Read and Write.* Westport, CT: Boynton/Cook, 1989.

———. *Learning by Teaching: Selected Articles on Writing and Teaching.* Westport, CT: Boynton/Cook, 1982.

Mutnick, Deborah. *Writing in an Alien World: Basic Writing and the Struggle for Equality in Higher Education.* Westport, CT: Boynton/Cook, 1995.

Ogbu, John. "Minority Status and Literacy in Comparative Perspective." *Daedalus* (1990): 141–168.

O'Reilley, Mary Rose. *Radical Presence: Teaching as a Contemplative Practice.* Westport, CT: Boynton/Cook, 1998.

Palmer, Parker J. *The Courage to Teach: Exploring the Inner Landscape of a Teacher's Life.* San Francisco, CA: Jossey-Bass Inc., 1997.

Scribner, Sylvia and Michael Cole. *The Psychology of Literacy.* Cambridge, MA:Harvard University Press, 1986.

Said, Edward. "Representing the Decolonized: Anthropology's Interlocutors." *Critical Inquiry* 15.2 (1980): 2–25.

Shaughnessy, Mina. *Errors and Expectations.* New York: Oxford University Press, 1977

Shor, Ira and Caroline Pari, eds. *Critical Literacy in Action: Writing Words, Changing Worlds.* Westport, CT: Boynton/Cook, 1999.

Shor, Ira. *Empowering Education: Critical Teaching for Social Change.* Chicago: University of Chicago Press, 1992.

Showalter, Elaine. "The Risks of Good Teaching: How 1 Professor and 9 T.A.'s Plunged into Pedagogy." *The Chronicle of Higher Education* 9 July: B4–6.

Smith, Maggie, *Teaching College Writing.* Needham Heights, MA: Allyn and Bacon, 1995

Snyder, Ilana. *Hypertext: the Electronic Labyrinth.* New York: New York University Press,1997.

Starkey, David, ed. *Teaching Writing Creatively.* Westport, CT: Boynton/Cook, 1998.

Street, Brian V. *Cross Cultural Approaches to Literacy.* Cambridge, MA: Cambridge University Press, 1993.

Stuckey, J. Elspeth. *The Violence of Literacy.* Portsmouth, NH: Boynton/Cook, 1991.

Tannen, Deborah, ed. *Gender and Conversation Interaction.* New York: Oxford University Press, 1993.

Tompkins, Jane. *A Life in School: What the Teacher Learned.* New York: Addison-Wesley, 1996.

Weaver, Constance, ed. *Lessons to Share on Teaching Grammar in Context.* Westport, CT: Boynton/Cook, 1998.

Weaver, Constance. *Teaching Grammar in Context.* Westport, CT: Boynton/Cook, 1996.

Welch, Anthony R. and Peter Freebody, eds. *Knowledge, Culture, and Power: International Perspectives on Literacy as Policy and Practice.* Pittsburgh, PA: University of Pittsburgh Press, 1993.

Young, Art and Toby Fulwiler, eds. *When Writing Teachers Teach Literature: Bringing Writing to Reading.* Westport, CT: Boynton/Cook, 1995.

ELECTRONIC

The Chronicle of Higher Education
http://chronicle.com/index.htm

Harcourt College Publishers
http://www.hbcollege.com/

Modern Language Association
http://www.mla.org/

National Council for Teachers of English
http://www.ncte.org/

National Writing Project
http://www-gse.berkeley.edu/Research/NWP/nwp.html

WPA: Council of Writing Program Administrators
http://www.cas.ilstu.edu/English/Hesse/wpawelcome.htm